CHARLES DE FOUCAULD

In the Footsteps of
Jesus of Nazareth

CHARLES DE FOUCAULD

In the Footsteps of
Jesus of Nazareth

A Biography

Annie of Jesus

New City Press
Hyde Park, NY

Published in the United States by New City Press
202 Cardinal Rd., Hyde Park, NY 12538
(first published in English by New City, London)
©2004 Little Sisters of Jesus (Engl. translation)

Translated by the Little Sisters of Jesus
from the original French edition
Charles de Foucauld: Sur les pas de Jésus de Nazareth
©2001 Nouvelle Cité

Cover design by Nick Cianfarani/Miguel Tejerina

Library of Congress Cataloging-in-Publication Data:

Annie, Little Sister of Jesus.
    Charles de Foucauld : in the footsteps of Jesus of Nazareth / by Little
Sister Annie of Jesus ; foreword by Ian Lathan.
        p. cm.
    Includes bibliographical references.
    ISBN 1-56548-229-8 (alk. paper)
    1. Foucauld, Charles de, 1858-1916. 2. Catholics--Biography. I. Title.
    BX4705.F65A56   2005
    271'.79-dc22

                                            2005004082

Printed in the United States of America

Contents

Preface

Charles de Foucauld was born in the mid-19th century into an old aristocratic French family. He spent the key years of his life in the Sahara desert as a Christian "monk" among the local Tuareg people, who were followers of Islam. There he met his death in 1916, in the central Saharan oasis of Tamanrasset.

What, we can well ask, has he to say to us? We live in a world far removed from his, and our personal lives, whatever they may be, surely hardly resemble his. And yet, surprisingly, his life has had a profound influence on many today. People of all kinds have discovered through him "a word of life" that gives meaning to their everyday lives, and a little sign of hope to encourage them on their journey.

The French society in which Charles was born and grew up was marked by strong, often bitter, class distinctions. In theory the French Revolution, with its famous slogan of "Liberté, Egalité, Fraternité" (derived from the United States' struggle for independence), had abolished these distinctions. In fact the old feudal order, with its clear social hierarchy and its integration of Church and State, was replaced by new class divisions linked to the industrial revolution. The old feudal loyalties were replaced by the harsh economic laws of "hire and fire": the worker became a "hired hand," to be employed or laid aside, as needed.

This social context helps us to grasp the radical nature of Charles' desire to imitate Jesus as the "workman of Nazareth." Was not Jesus the "carpenter"? This, Charles reminds us, is a truth we had largely forgotten! And had he not chosen to be at the bottom of the social ladder, in "the lowest place"?

Accompanying industrialization, the western European powers engaged in a massive colonial expansion, especially in Africa. This led, inevitably, to an open or latent hostility between the new "rulers," the colonizing military and civil authorities, and the "ruled," the local peoples. It was in this situation that Charles wished to be "the universal brother," a brother to each and every person he encountered. Such a simple and bold claim strikes at the heart of inhuman structures and relationships, and begins to remake a world of respect and equality. Charles did this not by words — he, as we do, mistrusted mere words — but by simple, everyday actions and gestures, with a readiness, when need be, to denounce abuses and take risks.

Work, especially manual work, was also looked down on by the Tuareg nobles. While few of us realize that the Sahara is even inhabited, the Tuareg, with whom Charles lived for over ten years, were a large but scattered group of nomadic peoples in the central Sahara, with an elaborate class structure. They have a rich and ancient culture and a deep faith, that of Islam. As Charles came to realize by sharing their life and studying their culture in detail, they looked down on the French occupants as "pagans" and as "barbarians." (Most of the French, even if nominally

Christian, did not express or practice their faith.) The Tuareg saw them as people with superior force of arms and material, technological means but with no sense of authentic values such as hospitality, freedom and courage.

Reading Charles' letters and personal reflections, we discover his own struggles to "see through" the ingrained, largely unconscious opinions of national and religious superiority, and to begin to see the different, but equally real worth of the "other." As the French settlers came to bring "civilization" and "Christianity," so perhaps we in today's West are tempted as neo-colonialists to offer, even impose, "free trade and democracy" as well as our modern religion of "secular humanism." Let us allow Charles to challenge us! How sadly we deform the real values and truths that are ours, and close ourselves to the truth and goodness of those different from ourselves!

It is perhaps fortunate that Charles lost his Christian faith in adolescence. By rediscovering it through the living example of his Muslim hosts (in Morocco especially), he was not tempted to despise the profound value of their religion, or its providential role in God's plan. Returning to his Christian faith as a mature adult, he never doubted its God-given and absolute truth and he built his whole life, without reserve, around it. The lived example of Brother Charles — totally faithful to Jesus, totally respectful of God's ways in his neighbors — surely provides a light for us today, particularly in relation to Islam and the Muslim people.

As an adult Charles had little, in fact almost no, experience of the ordinary life of the French Church of his day. Soon after his discovery of faith he became a monk and left for a poor monastery in Syria. But the religious picture in France was complicated. There were the "Jansenists," who over-emphasized the judgment of God and the demand for ever stricter moral standards. There were the "Modernists," who over emphasized the application of human reason, tending to interpret religion in terms of our developing human history and psychology. And then there were the "Skeptics," those who denied the truth of any religious belief. Those who remained in the Church were influenced by their criticisms and doubts, not unlike us in our own day. While these factors had played a role in Charles' loss of faith as an adolescent, it seems as though once he found a genuine adult faith, he never allowed himself to be pulled into factional disputes but went to the "center" of faith, the person of Jesus. He went always to the "heart of the matter," the unfathomable love of the one Source of all in the human life of Jesus, the man of Nazareth.

It must be added that the Catholic Church in France was also under attack at this time from the secular society. Many of its institutions had been closed, properties seized and most religious orders were disbanded. The very presence of missionaries in the colonies was barely tolerated. This had an important effect on the ability of the Church to confront certain social structures both at home and abroad, not the least of which was the question of slavery. Although Charles' military connections, as a former French officer and explorer, gave him a certain privileged access to the Saharan territories, he refused to be a "dumb sentinel" but protested with vigor against the institution and practice of slavery.

On his return from exploring the interior of Morocco Charles wrote a book which became a best seller. If then he was known in his day as an "explorer," we can also see that his whole life was an "exploration." Having discovered Jesus, he sought to discover who this Jesus really was. Visiting the little town of Nazareth, he suddenly became aware that Jesus had lived and worked in this ordinary, out-of-the-way place as a manual worker for some thirty years, in fact for all but three years of his life. If God became "one of us," as he firmly believed, was it not extraordinary that God had chosen to enter our human history in this apparently "insignificant" way? A way that is "our" way: the way that most of us live, the way of our common experience.

Charles explored and developed this insight for the rest of his life. It is the hidden "key" that opens the door to our understanding of Charles' life, and to the interest and importance of the "message" that his life may have for each of us.

We can easily be absorbed by the dramatic and picturesque life of Charles as the intrepid explorer, risking his life, and then as the solitary "hermit in the Sahara." During this time of exploration he already wanted to get to know, understand and to be with the local people. On his return as a priest, he sought to found a "fraternity," a community of brothers who would live his ideal of universal brotherhood. His conception of being a brother to one and all was not just a human ideal, but the lived consequence of Charles' deep belief that God had come to share our life and to live as one of us, to be "our Brother."

Our faith is so often separate from our daily life and choices. For Charles, to follow Jesus was to become "like Jesus," and to act like Jesus with every person and in every situation.

Of course we don't, most of us, live in the desert! Nor do we live in Charles' world or share his limited need of food and sleep, nor his almost boundless energy. But through him we can, each of us, whatever our situation, find inspiration — a "breath of the Spirit," through him for our often empty lives.

This little book gives us all the material we need to get in touch with the inner workings of Brother Charles' life and, through him, with the living presence of Jesus, his constant Companion and Friend.

Ian Lathan
Little Brother of Jesus

Introduction

Charles de Foucauld was born in Strasbourg in 1858. The early loss of both father and mother, at the age of six, left a deep scar in the young child.

During a difficult adolescence, he lost his faith and, perhaps to compensate for the profound sadness that he bore in his heart, he plunged into a life of pleasure and disorder.

As a young army officer, aged twenty-two, he was sent to Algeria. Two years later, he left the army and undertook a risky exploration in Morocco. The witness of the Muslim faith awakened in him the question: "Does God exist?"

On his return to France, touched by the affectionate and discreet welcome of his deeply Christian family, he began to search for the truth, and he met, providentially, a priest who became for him a father and a friend: Abbé Huvelin. In October 1886 at the age of 28, he converted.

From this moment, he wanted to give his whole life to God. A pilgrimage in the Holy Land revealed to him the figure of Jesus of Nazareth: a figure that fascinated him, a figure he would follow and imitate. He spent, first of all, seven years in a Trappist monastery, and then four years in Nazareth, as a hermit at the door of a Poor Clare convent. Progressively, he discovered that to follow Jesus and to love him passionately involved coming close to those who are far off, those who are "most abandoned."

Ordained priest in 1901, he left for the Sahara, settling first at Beni Abbès and then at Tamanrasset, with the aim simply of becoming the friend and brother of the desert nomads, through learning their language and entering into their culture. He did not seek to convert but to love, wishing to "cry the Gospel" throughout the whole of his life.

On 1 December 1916, in the Hoggar (central Sahara), he died, assassinated. It was during the First World War, and he had chosen to remain to the end among his friends.

There are many biographies about this man of God who has marked out, for thousands of disciples, an authentic Gospel way.

This book, made up of extracts from his writings, is a little initiation into his spirituality. Its aim is simply to give the reader a taste to go further and to discover more of "Brother Charles of Jesus," as he came to call himself.

As he wrote to one of his childhood friends: "Imitation is inseparable from love: it's the secret of my life. I've lost my heart for this Jesus of Nazareth, crucified one thousand nine hundred years ago, and I spend my life trying to imitate Him, as best as my weakness allows."[1]

No one who begins to listen to Brother Charles can remain indifferent, for his life and writings bring us back again and again to the living Person of Jesus and to His message.

He will, I hope, draw us too along the steps of this Jesus of Nazareth, his "Beloved Brother and Lord."

The Years of Unbelief
and the Path to Conversion

Childhood and Teenage Years

Charles de Foucauld was born on 15 September 1858, in Strasbourg, in the Province of Alsace, on the border between France and Germany. Twelve years later Alsace would be annexed by Germany as a prize in the War of 1870.

The Foucauld family, rich and aristocratic, had a long-standing military tradition.

When Charles reminisced about his childhood, he rarely mentioned his father, an inspector of forests and waterways who lived away from the family because he was quite ill. But with emotion he would often speak of the tender affection and the piety of his mother.

> From babyhood I was surrounded by so many graces, son of a holy mother, who taught me to know you, to love you and to pray to you as soon as I could babble.[1]

But he was not to enjoy this maternal presence for long. Very early, tragedy struck his life. The pain of losing both mother and father within the space of a few months left the six-year-old boy with wounds that took years to heal.

Charles' maternal grandfather took him under his care. A few years later, a new grief struck his life: when war broke out in 1870 he had to flee before the German invasion, for Strasbourg was close to the border. After France's defeat, Charles' grandfather chose to settle in Nancy, in the neighboring province of Lorraine, which had remained French.

At the age of twelve, Charles was already an orphan and a refugee. These losses left him with painful inner emptiness. On the threshold of adolescence, he kept to himself, an uncommunicative, sensitive, troubled boy.

He had an intelligent, inquiring mind and developed an early passion for reading. He grew up in a historical period marked by religious skepticism and philosophies that accepted only scientific facts as truth. People believed that science alone could find answers to the great questions of human existence. Before long Charles had lost his faith. He himself said that for twelve years he remained an unbeliever.

> By the time I was 15 or 16 I had no trace of faith left. The books I used to devour had done this to me. I didn't subscribe to any specific philosophy, as none of them seemed solidly proved enough to me. I doubted everything, especially the Catholic faith, since there were several of its dogmas that I found insulting to reason.[2]

More or less unconsciously he was searching for a true reason to live. Like many young people today, he despaired of finding a deep meaning to life.

Later he wrote to his cousin about this period of his life:

I was nothing but selfishness, irreverence, immorality. I went wild.[3]

His letters to his childhood friend, Gabriel Tourdes, show a need for immediate gratification, a kind of frenzy for life, as if to rid himself of his agonizing interior distress.

> Dear old Tourdes, it's been a long time since I wrote to you. I'm coming on Friday. I want to warn you I'll be counting on you every night. We'll go back to our reading with a rage. I'm furiously happy about coming back to Nancy for a while. I'm planning to enjoy myself completely, body and mind.[4]

He was 20 when he finished officer training at the military school of Saint Cyr, but his career in the army lasted only three years.

His grandfather had just died. The great effect his grief had on him shows his deep sensitivity.

> At Nancy an immense sorrow befell me. I lost my grandfather. I admired his high intelligence, and his inexhaustible affection had enfolded my youth and childhood in an atmosphere of love. I can still feel the warmth of it and it always moves me. His death hurt me terribly, and fourteen years later [it was 3 February 1878 that he died] the pain is still sharp.[5]

From that time on nothing held him back. To fill the emptiness in his heart, he threw himself into a life of worldly pleasure, all the easier since he had a great deal of money.

> I fell into a disorderly life and lived that way a long time, though it didn't kill off my fondness for study. In the regiment I ran wild, since none of my family were around. I saw scarcely anyone from my family between 1878 and

1886. What little they knew of my life, especially at the beginning of those years, can only have distressed them.[6]

After his conversion, Brother Charles looked at this part of his life again, under the light of faith. His did not aim to dwell on the past but to sing a hymn to God's mercy.

With a sense of wonder he discovered that when he had been straying far from God, refusing to believe in him, when he had been sunk in sin, God had always been there waiting for him, seeking him, guiding him with infinite love, though he did not realize it.

> I was going further and further from you, my Lord and my Life. And so my life was turning into death. And in this state of death, you still watched over me. You made me feel a painful emptiness, a sadness the like of which I've never felt before or since. It came over me every night when I went home to my lodgings. What we called our festivities left me silent and heavy-hearted. You gave me the vague restlessness of a troubled conscience, for though my conscience was asleep it was not altogether dead. I have never felt that sadness, that ill ease, that restlessness at any time but then. It must have been your gift, my God. I was far from suspecting this. How good you are! How you kept me safe! How you sheltered me under your wings when I didn't even believe you existed![7]

Brother Charles' own painful experience of sin led him to the conviction that God loves people unconditionally with a love altogether freely given. And because God loves each of his creatures so passionately, God had never stopped waiting for him, seeking him, looking after him all the years he was astray.

> My God, how good you are! At the very moment when you punished Adam, you offered him hope, the hope of

the greatest glory and the greatest happiness. You let him see from afar the "seed" and the blessed woman by whom the serpent's head would be crushed. How good you are, my God, and how unchanging. You who do not break the crushed reed or quench the wavering flame.

And isn't this exactly what you still do every day? Don't you call to us by the voice of your Church and tell us that whatever our sins, however long our unfaithfulness has lasted, we need only return to you and repent and we will be saved? You will not only deliver us from every evil but make us heirs to all glory and all happiness. No sinner is so great, no wrong-doer so hardened, but you will offer him Paradise at the top of your voice, as you did to the good thief in response to a mere moment's good will.[8]

Brother Charles' conviction speaks to us today. People often talk about the absence of God. Is not the place where God seems absent precisely the place where God is? Doesn't God remain mysteriously present in the hearts of those who reject him, as he does in those who worship him?

This is what the great prophets of the Old Testament were talking about: "Does a woman forget her baby at the breast or fail to cherish the child of her womb? Yet even if these forget, I will never forget you. I have branded you on the palms of my hands." [Is 49:15–16]

How are we to answer for our faith today except to bear witness to it right in the deserts of the world? By our whole lives we bear witness to the unfathomable love of God for every human being, especially for those whom the world abandons, excludes, gives up on.

The Path to Conversion

As the nineteenth century drew to a close, France was carving out a vast colonial empire in Africa and Asia.

In 1830, France had begun the conquest of Algeria. After occupying and annexing the whole territory, the French army stayed on to administer the southern territories, including the Saharan oases.

Thus, in 1881 Charles, a young officer of 23, was sent to the garrison of Setif. He arrived accompanied by a young lady he had taken up with, who he tried at first to pass off as his wife. Several times, his commanding officers ordered him to break off with her, but he refused. As a consequence, he was charged with insubordination and notorious conduct, and was removed from active duty.

Overnight he was back in France.

He did not defy authority because of his attachment to the young woman, for just as abruptly a few months later, he left her. But his fierce independence prevented him from accepting any limit to his freedom. Nobody had the right to make him give in.

A few weeks later, as he was whiling away his time in Evian, he learned that his regiment was taking part in operations in Tunisia. Instantly he applied to be reinstated and was assigned to a regiment in Southern Algeria, where an uprising had arisen.

Why this turnaround? A taste for adventure and danger was probably the chief factor, as shown in this letter to G. Tourdes:

> An expedition like this is too rare a pleasure. I can't let it go by without trying to get in on the fun.[9]

But wasn't something else involved, less consciously perhaps: an upsurge of generosity, a feeling of solidarity?

As soon as he arrived to take part in the expedition he showed himself

> just as able to put up with privation and fatigue as he had put up with pleasure. Unfailingly in good spirits, he bore hunger and even thirst cheerfully. He was good to his men, always looking for ways to make things better for them and sharing their lot completely.[10]

The vast spaces of southern Algeria fascinated Charles de Foucauld. He fell in love with Africa.

Once again, a few months later, he quit the army, this time for good. He wanted to stay where he was and began carefully to prepare himself to explore Morocco.

Under a false identity as a fellow rabbi, he traveled into the Kingdom of Morocco with the learned Rabbi Mardochee. He braved many dangers, since Morocco had closed itself to Europeans, forbidding them to enter.

He had gone to Algeria as a member of a conquering army. He could enter Morocco only as one of the poor, disguised as an outcast Jew.

For nearly a year, from June 1883 to May 1884, he experienced poverty and social stigma, things that had never touched him before. His friend, the explorer Duvreyier, later said that during his trip Charles "made a vow of poverty and destitution, and more than kept it."

It was an experience he would never forget.

As he shared the life of the Jewish communities who gave him hospitality, he took part in their Sabbath prayers.

Traveling without defense in a strange land, totally dependent on those who took him under their roof, he could have been killed at any moment. Twice his Muslim or Jewish hosts saw through his disguise. He came out alive only because they were believers and held the life of a guest sacred. Charles never forgot these heights of hospitality.

He saw Muslims at their daily prayers, and their testimony of prayer affected him:

> Islam made a very deep impression on me. The sight of such faith, of people living continually in the presence of God, made me glimpse something greater and truer than worldly pursuits. I set about studying Islam, and then the Bible.[11]

It was not Christians, then, who awakened Charles' religious yearnings, but other believers, fellow children of Abraham. God alone holds the secret of such mysterious connections.

Charles stayed in Algiers during 1885, writing up his travel notes. He had frequent contacts with Commandant Titre, a geographer who had a 23-year-old daughter. An affection soon sprang up between Charles and Marguerite, and in May 1885, they decided to announce their engagement. Charles wrote to her:

> I shall leave you free to do as you like in religious matters, but as for myself I shan't go to church, as I do not have the faith.[12]

At the end of May Charles returned to France and found his family dead-set against the engagement. A few months later he decided to break it off. Doing it cost him a lot, especially, so it seems, at the thought of the pain he was imposing on the young woman, who was very fond of him.

His trip through Morocco had left him far more mature, and had made him famous.

His family welcomed him warmly. It touched him deeply that they made no moralistic allusions to his stormy past.

They just expressed their joy at having him back, like a prodigal son.

Those who welcomed him most were his sister and his cousin Marie. They didn't hide the fact that they were Christians. They asked Charles no questions, but he began to feel stirrings of his own.

> When I was in Paris, I found myself among people who were very intelligent, very virtuous and deeply Christian. I told myself that this religion might not be so absurd after all.[13]

The watchful, unobtrusive presence of his cousin, Marie de Bondy, for whom Charles kept a deep bond of affection all his life, touched him greatly. He was grateful most of all for her discretion:

> She seconded your work, my God, by her silence, her gentleness and her goodness. She was kind, but she didn't intervene.[14]

The Return of the Prodigal

The young explorer was still searching. Indifferent to the glowing praises of the Geographical Society for his work in Morocco, he turned his attention elsewhere. His unbelief had yielded to uncertainty and he began searching sincerely for the truth.

He started by immersing himself in classical philosophy, but became disenchanted. He then began reading a book his cousin Marie de Bondy had given him, Bossuet's *Elévations sur les Mystères*, a commentary on the Gospel of John. Reading it made him begin to realize that he could not reach God through his own will power, for God is not an idea to master but a person to encounter.

And so, like someone groping in the dark, he went looking for that encounter. He set his heart on it. This was the turning point he would call "the dawn of my conversion" in a meditation on the parable of the prodigal son.

> Your first grace, the one I see as the dawn of my conversion, was to have given me a hunger. It was then I came back to you, timidly groping my way, and repeating this strange prayer: "If you exist, then let me know you."[15]

The lost son at last had heard the Father's call that echoes through the centuries, ever since Genesis: "Adam, where are you?"

Months went by. The one who would be the instrument of Charles' encounter with God, Father Huvelin, entered his story.[16]

This priest, trained as a historian and a specialist in classical Greek, had chosen to remain a curate at the church of Saint Augustine in Paris, refusing any higher post. For 35 years he exercised his apostolate as a priest.

His fragile health gave him a heightened sensitivity to the suffering of others. He welcomed, comforted and transformed many penitents. Crowds flocked to hear his sermons.

Although well aware of the modernist controversy that was dividing the French Church, he took no part in it. He simply made himself available as a friend and confidant to those who found themselves torn between their deepest convictions and some of the Church's decisions.

Marie de Bondy, one of Fr. Huvelin's parishioners, had spoken about him to her cousin. Charles later wrote:

> Lord, when you made me enter his confessional on one of the last days in October 1886, you gave me everything. If there is joy in heaven when a sinner repents, then there

must have been some when I entered that confessional. I asked for religious instruction. He told me to kneel down and make my confession.[17]

Fr. Huvelin answered this young man he barely knew, and who was asking to discuss religion with him, with a point blank invitation to conversion: bring the truth into your inmost heart by acknowledging yourself as a sinner and "come to the light."

Only when our hearts are broken in sorrow for our sins can God make them new again as "hearts of flesh."

Charles hesitated a moment at the invitation. Then, without arguing, he obeyed. The man who had never deigned to bend his will to someone else knelt down, acknowledged his faults and experienced the inexpressible joy of the prodigal son. Ten years later, writing at Nazareth, he recalled that moment:

> How good is the prodigal son's father. But you were a thousand times more generous than he. You did a thousand times more for me than he for his son. How good you are my Lord and my God!
>
> When I was that prodigal son, I was not just welcomed with unspeakable kindness and without punishment, without reprimand, with no reminders of the past. I was not just welcomed with kisses, with the finest robe and a signet ring as a child of the house. Not just all that, but my blessed Father came looking for me and brought me back from the faraway country.[18]

In the same text he speaks of the Eucharist:

> And how divine was the banquet you have invited me to, so much beyond the banquet for the prodigal son. You brought me in to that banquet immediately.[19]

Charles was conscious of being poor and a sinner. In this frame of mind he met the God of Love, who forgives without limit, who is always out looking for the lost sheep. And under the sign of broken bread, he already had a glimpse of the one who came as a poor man to encounter our human race, and who is always there among us walking with us.

Charles had found his faith, but as he himself admitted:

> At the beginning, this faith of mine had many obstacles to overcome. I had doubted for so long, I didn't believe everything in a day. Sometimes it was the miracles in the Gospels I found unbelievable, sometimes I wanted to mix passages from the Koran in with my prayers. But divine grace and the advice of my confessor blew the fog away.[20]

Before long, he would experience something like what Paul meant when he wrote to the Corinthians: "If anyone is in Christ, he is a new creation." [2 Cor 5:17]

A few years later Charles wrote:

> It is so true that the just live by faith, for faith replaces most of our natural senses. Through our senses we perceive nothing but deceptive appearances; sight shows us a poor person; faith shows us Jesus. The ear makes us hear insults and threats; faith sings to us, "rejoice and be glad." Touch makes us feel rocks thrown at us; faith tells us, "Be glad you have had the honor of suffering something for Christ's name." Taste tells us it is a little unleavened bread; faith shows us "Jesus the Savior." Our senses love wealth and prestige; faith detests them: "What people think highly of is loathsome in the sight of God" ... "Happy are the poor." And faith reveres the poverty and the lowliness in which Jesus clothed his whole life, like a garment that could not be removed. The senses recoil from suffering; faith blesses it as a gift from the hand of

Jesus, a share in his cross that he deigns to let us carry with him.

And so the just who live by faith have their souls full of new ideas, new pleasures, new principles. New horizons open out in front of them, marvelous horizons illumined by a heavenly light whose beauty comes from the beauty of God. Absorbed in these new truths that the world has no notion of, believers have no choice but to start a new life. Anyone who sees this light and takes it at its true value holds it infinitely important, clings to it unshakably, follows it in everything and refuses to be turned aside by anything.[21]

Acutely aware of having been saved, brought back to life by the mercy of God, Charles felt an immense trust and an immense love spring up in his heart. He based his trust on what Jesus said to the woman weeping at his feet in the house of Simon the Pharisee: "I tell you, her sins, her many sins, must have been forgiven her or she would not have shown such great love. It is the one who is forgiven little who shows little love." [Lk 7:47] Charles would cite this text again when he wrote to Fr. Huvelin to submit his first foundation projects to him.[22] And because his experience went so deep, he never forgot he was a pardoned sinner and that "the Son of Man came to seek out and save what was lost." [Lk 19:10]

> We can hope. We are precisely the ones Jesus came to save, for we are being lost. Yes, without him we are perishing at every moment. We can hope, for whatever we may be guilty of, Jesus wants to save us. The more sinful we are, the closer to death, the deeper our state of despair for our body and our soul, the more it can be said that Jesus wants to save us, for he came to save what was about to be lost. We must never be discouraged but always

hope. We are on the edge of a gulf, we are about to sink, we deserve to sink, we truly ought to sink because of our measureless ingratitude, we are sinking. We are just the ones Jesus came to save. He wants to save us because we are sinking. He is infinitely good and infinitely powerful. To the very last, as long as there is a breath of life left, all can hope in him.[23]

He often repeated that it was those who were the least whom Jesus chose, not only to save them but also to make them his special friends:

"He saw Levi sitting by the customs house." [Mk 2:14] There is no state so contemptible, so worthy of contempt, where you cannot reach in and pull people out, not only to save them but to make them your favorites, to raise them to great holiness. You reach down into the dust of the road to recover lost coins that people have been trampling on, and make them shine like new. We must never lose hope, not for ourselves or for others or for anyone, no matter how sunk in vice. Someone may seem to have choked off the last shred of goodness inside, but we must never lose hope, not only that such a one not only may be saved but even may climb the heights of holiness. God is mighty enough to do it. The Good Shepherd can bring sheep back to his fold at the eleventh hour as at the first hour. His goodness, like his power, has no limits. To be always ready to hope is an obligation for us.[24]

Later, Brother Charles would find the words to communicate this strong hope in God's mercy with great understanding and kindness to people tormented by a sense of their wretchedness, as in this letter to his friend L. Massignon:

Peace and trust. Hope. Don't dwell on yourself. Our moral wretchedness is a muddy swamp that should often inspire us to humble ourselves, but we shouldn't always have our eyes on it. We should also turn our eyes to the Beloved, and keep them much more often on him, on his beauty and his infinite love with which he graciously loves us. When you love you forget yourself and think of the one you love. If we're constantly thinking of how unworthy of being loved we are, that's not love.[25]

Captivated by Jesus of Nazareth

A Fascination with the Incarnation

Probably in 1888 Charles heard a phrase in one of Fr. Huvelin's sermons which, as he later said, was to "engrave itself indelibly in my soul":

> Jesus took the last place so utterly that no one has ever been able to get it away from him.

At about the same time, the end of 1888, Fr. Huvelin urged him to go on pilgrimage to the Holy Land. Why? Perhaps because he sensed that this explorer was a man to whom places meant a lot. Before he would be able to understand his faith better with his mind, he would need to see and touch something. This is just what happened. While in the places where the Incarnation actually came about, Brother Charles had a powerful insight into how real it was. It is a bit like what Saint Thomas said: he needed to see with his own eyes and touch with his hands just how much God had loved us, just how much he had become one of us, poor among the poor.

Arriving in Palestine in December, he went first to Bethlehem to spend Christmas. There, from his weakness and poverty the tiny baby of the manger reached out to him:

> After spending Christmas 1888 at Bethlehem and hearing midnight Mass and receiving Holy Communion at the grotto, two or three days later I went back to Jerusalem. The sweetness I had felt praying in that grotto where the voices of Jesus, Mary and Joseph once echoed and where I was so close to them had been inexpressible. But it took only an hour's walk, and the church of the Holy Sepulchre, Calvary and the Mount of Olives loomed up ahead of me. Whether I wanted it or not, my thoughts had to change direction so I could be there at the foot of the Cross.[1]

A few days later at the beginning of January, he arrived at Nazareth. There he discovered, as he wrote to one of his cousins, "the humble, obscure existence of the divine workman of Nazareth."[2]

Going to Nazareth had a decisive impact. The shock echoed in his heart like a call. The vocation it awakened in him would express itself in an ever-intensifying desire. Seven years later as he was leaving the Trappists, he wrote:

> I am thirsting to lead at last the life I've been looking for these seven years and more. I glimpsed it, guessed at it, as I was walking the streets of Nazareth where the feet of Our Lord had trod, a poor craftsman lost in extreme lowliness and obscurity.[3]

Charles' route now took on a direction. Charles had been captured by the mystery of God's humility and throughout his life he would never stop contemplating it.

Meditating on the birth of Jesus, he wrote on 6 November 1897:

> The Incarnation takes its source from God's goodness. But there is one thing about it so marvelous that it shines like a dazzling sign: the infinite humility such a mystery contains. God, the Infinite, the Almighty, becomes human, the least of all human beings. For myself, let me always seek the last place of all, so that I can be as lowly as my master. I must walk with him step by step as his faithful disciple and live with my God who lived his whole life in the last place and gave me such an example of this in his birth.[4]

And he added directly afterwards:

> "He went down with them and came to Nazareth and lived under their authority." You went down to live the life of poor working people, toiling for their living ... at Nazareth.[5]

To speak of "the last place" and "extreme lowliness" for Jesus' life at Nazareth may seem exaggerated. Charles was probably influenced by his times. Especially in the social classes he came from, aristocrats looked down upon manual work. Besides that, Nazareth, then under Turkish rule, would have seemed squalid to the eyes of a traveler from Paris.

But perhaps we should look deeper and remember that he had just been to Bethlehem, then to Jerusalem. What had such impact on him was to realize that Jesus had chosen to take on the conditions of the poor from his birth to his death. He would turn to this discovery for inspiration all

through his life, as we see from this meditation written in
June 1916, at Tamanrasset:

> "He went down with them and came to Nazareth": all his
> life he did nothing but go down. He went down when he
> took flesh, he went down by becoming a little baby, he
> went down by obeying, he went down by becoming poor,
> abandoned, outcast, persecuted, tortured, taking always
> and everywhere the last place.[6]

The central insight of Brother Charles' faith is here. It is
in profound harmony with the heart of Christian revela-
tion. How can we keep from thinking of the Suffering Servant in Isaiah? The Apostles keep referring to this Servant
in their early preaching. Paul too has this in mind in the Servant hymn in the letter to the Philippians.

The Way of Discipleship

Thus Charles' pilgrimage to the Holy Land can be summed up as a fascination with a person. It is not so much an
event that can be marked on a calendar, but rather a call.
The inner energies this call awoke would show themselves
throughout Charles' life.

The God who had revealed himself to him in the figure of
Jesus of Nazareth now drew Charles to leave everything and
follow him:

> The Gospel showed me that the first commandment is to
> love God with all one's heart and that love had to be the
> beginning and the end of everything. Everybody knows
> that the first effect of love is imitation. So what I had to
> do next was to enter the Order where I could find the
> closest imitation of Jesus. I didn't feel I was made for
> preaching like Jesus in his public life, so I needed to

imitate him in his hidden life as a poor and humble workman at Nazareth. I thought nothing would offer me this
way of life better than a Trappist monastery.[7]

Charles' motives are clear: because of Jesus and his Gospel, he wanted to take up the way of discipleship and let
Jesus take possession of him and lead him on.

> Why did I enter the Trappists? Out of love, pure love. I
> love our Lord Jesus Christ, though I wish my heart could
> love him better and more. Still, I love him and I cannot
> bear to lead a life different from his. I do not want a com-
> fortable, respected life when his was the hardest and most
> reviled that ever was.[8]

Charles clearly felt that following in the footsteps of Jesus
of Nazareth required him to become quite concretely poor
the way his master had been:

> My God, I do not know if some people can see you poor
> and willingly remain rich. Can they realize they are so
> much above their master, their Beloved, and not want to
> be like you in every way within their power, to be like you
> most of all in your lowliness? I'm sure they must love you,
> my God, but I think there's something missing in their
> love. In any case, I for my part cannot conceive a love
> without a need, a compelling need, to be alike, to do the
> same, and most of all to share all the hardships and trials
> and troubles of life. To be rich and secure and live com-
> fortably off my property, when you were poor and needy
> and toiled for your living. As for me, I couldn't do it, my
> God. I couldn't love like that. The servant should not be
> greater than his master.[9]

On 15 January 1890, he said good-bye to his family, part-
ing from his cousin Marie with his heart breaking. He

arrived at the Trappist Monastery of Our Lady of the Snows on 16 January.

A few months later, he was sent to another monastery, recently founded at Akbes in Syria (under Turkish rule). The buildings were makeshift and life was harder there. Brother Marie Alberic (his religious name as a Trappist) was happy.

But nostalgia for Nazareth was not slow in coming back. Soon he was writing to Fr. Huvelin:

> You hope I've poverty enough. No, we are poor in comparison with the rich, but we are not as poor as our Lord was, not poor the way I was in Morocco, not poor like Saint Francis.[10]

One day he was sent to keep vigil at the bedside of a poor Catholic who was dying in a small village nearby. He reflected:

> What a difference between this house and where I live. I pine for Nazareth.[11]

A desire began to grow in his heart then. Since no order offered the poverty and the form of life he was dreaming of, why not found a little religious congregation which would have no other aim but to live a life like Jesus at Nazareth?

He brought it up to Fr. Huvelin in 1893:

> Wouldn't it be possible to form a little congregation to lead this life? We would live only from the work of our own hands, like our Lord, who did not take up collections or live from offerings, nor did he have foreign laborers working for him while he sat back and supervised. Couldn't a few people be found to follow our Lord like this, to follow him by following all his counsels? They would renounce all ownership of property, whether

collective or individual, and consequently they could absolutely forbid themselves what our Lord prohibited: all lawsuits, accusations, and defense of their rights. They would make it an absolute duty to give alms: if they have two habits they must give one of them away: if they have something to eat they must give some to those who have nothing, and not keep anything for the next day. They would follow all the examples of Jesus' hidden life and all the counsels that came from his lips.

It would be a life of work and prayer, not with two categories of religious as the Trappists have, but only one, as Saint Benedict wanted it to be. There would just be long silent prayer, the rosary, the holy Mass. Our liturgy closes the door on Arabs, Turks, Armenians and such, who are good Catholics but do not know a word of our languages. I would so like to see little nests like these set up, and in them a fervent and hard-working life, reproducing the life of our Lord, under his keeping and with the protection of Mary and Joseph. There should be one near every mission in the East, where life is so isolated. It would offer a refuge to the souls of the people in these countries whom God calls to serve him and to love him single-heartedly.

Is this a dream, dear Father? Is it an illusion from the devil or is it an idea and an invitation that comes from God? If I could be sure it came from God, I would start on it today and not tomorrow and do what I need to do to take up this path. When I think about the concept, I find it ideal. But when I think about the one who conceived it, and conceived it so ardently, I do not think I see in him the stuff God usually uses to do good things. It is true that if I made a start, then if the project came from God he would be the one to give the increase. Something else gives me courage to undertake a project so little suited to a sinner of my unworthiness: the Lord said that the one who had sinned greatly would be the one who should love greatly.[12]

He had spelled his project out clearly. And yet Brother Marie Alberic did not leave the Trappists until January 1897. Why did he wait so long?

This was a man of impulsive, impatient nature, who wanted to put the ideas he conceived into action immediately. But there was a single desire taking hold of him more and more: to let himself be led by the Will of God. And so, for this decisive step he would wait for God's will to be confirmed for him by Fr. Huvelin and by his Trappist superiors. He trusted that he would find his path through them.

Perhaps he also vaguely guessed that he first had to surrender this project so dear to him to God, to make a sacrifice of it, one might say.

The meditation he wrote just at this time on the sacrifice of Abraham may reveal what was going on in his own heart:

> Saint Abraham, blessed are you. Saint Isaac, who let yourself be tied to the altar without resistance, blessed are you. My God, who plants such virtues in human beings, blessed are you for all ages without end.
>
> Love means obeying you, obeying you with just such promptness and such faith, though our heart is breaking and our mind in turmoil, though every idea we have held be turned upside down. Love means unrestricted, unhesitating sacrifice of what we hold most dear, to your Will. The sacrifice of the only son, of what our heart wants most. Love means trading all our desires for nothing but suffering, out of love for the Lord.
>
> This is what you did, Abraham. This is what you were to do, O Son of God, when you came down from heaven to earth to live the life you lived and die the death you died.

My Lord and my God, make me do the same and follow your Holy Will. Saint Abraham and Saint Isaac, pray
for me.[13]

In 1896, Fr. Huvelin agreed to Brother Marie Alberic's
plan. The date when he would have to either make his final
vows or leave the order was coming up. His superiors would
have to make a decision about him.

At this crucial moment at the end of 1896, he was feeling
a remarkable self-surrender. He asked for nothing and just
trusted God to take care of everything. We know this from a
letter he wrote to Brother Jerome, a young Trappist he had
met at the monastery of Staouëli and to whom he had been
asked to be like an older brother. He wrote to him first
about obedience:

> Obedience is the last, the highest and most perfect of the
> degrees of love. Here you cease to exist in yourself, you
> become nothing, you die as Jesus did on the Cross.[14]

And a little further on he wrote:

> I've had to practice obedience a lot just this week, and
> obedience is still what I have to practice, along with cour-
> age.
>
> For the last three and a half years I've been asking to
> pass from the status of choir monk to that of lay brother,
> either in the Order or in another religious order with
> houses in the East. I think this is my vocation: to go
> down.
>
> With the permission of my confessor, I had submitted
> this request. My superiors ordered me, before they would
> grant it, to go and spend some time at Staouëli. When I
> got there, to my great surprise I was told to go to Rome.
> And here I thought I would have to wait a long time still
> before I was given the permission I longed for. But our

good Father General has called me in, examined my motives, reflected on my vocation, called together his Council, and they all unanimously agree that the Will of God is for me to follow this path of lowliness, poverty and humble manual labor, life as a workman of Nazareth that the Workman of Nazareth himself has been inspiring in me for so long. I got the news yesterday from our dear, wonderful Father General, whose kindness touches me so much.

But the point where I had need of obedience was before his decision. I had promised God that I would do everything Reverend Father told me after the examination of my vocation he was about to undertake and everything my confessor told me to do. So if they had said to me, "You will make your solemn vows in ten days" and later on "You will be ordained a priest," I would have obeyed with joy, sure that I was doing the will of God. For I was seeking absolutely nothing but the will of God, and I had superiors who were seeking only his will too. So it was impossible that God would not make his will known.[15]

On 23 January 1897, he was thus given permission to leave the Trappist Order.

On 14 February he made private vows in the presence of his confessor, a vow of perpetual chastity and a vow "never to have in his possession or at his disposal more than a poor workman would have."

And on 17 February, he set sail for the Holy Land. A few days later Fr. Huvelin wrote to him:

Yes, like you my dear child, I picture you in the East. I prefer Capernaum or Nazareth or some Franciscan convent, not in the convent, but in its shadow. Just ask to use the spiritual resources of the convent and live in poverty at the door. This, my dear friend, is what I can see possible.

Don't think about gathering followers around you and still less of giving them a rule. Live your life, and if followers come, live the same life together. But make no rules. On this I insist.[16]

From Nazareth to Beni Abbès

Hermit at Nazareth

The Poor Clares of Nazareth took Charles on as a hired man. He lived in a tool shed and christened it "Hermitage of our Lady of Perpetual Help."

He led a life still deeply marked by his recent experience in the monastery. He had more time than ever for reading, praying and meditating silently in the shelter of the cloister.

> You ask me for details about my life. I am staying in a solitary shed. It's inside the Sisters' enclosure and I am their happy servant. I am alone there. It is a gem of a hermitage, perfectly solitary. I get up when my Guardian Angel wakes me and I pray and meditate till time for the Angelus. Then I go over to the Franciscan convent and go down to the grotto that was part of the Holy Family's house. I stay there till about 6:00 in the morning, saying my rosary and hearing Masses. It delights me deeply to look at the rock walls that Jesus once had before his eyes and touched with his hands. At 6:00 I go back to the

Sisters, set up for their Mass and serve it at 7:00. Then I do whatever I am told to. If there's an errand I do it, but that's very rare. In general I spend my day doing odd jobs in my little room near the sacristy. I stay in the chapel from 5:00 to 7:30 in the evening. After that I go back to my dear hermitage. I read till 9:00 and go to bed. I read during the meals; I eat alone. I see nobody at all but my confessor once a week to go to confession and the Sisters when they have to tell me something, which happens rarely.[1]

Almost all Brother Charles' meditations on the Scriptures come from these years at Nazareth. He truly fed his prayer and his desire to be like Jesus "at the table of the Word as at the table of the Eucharist." His desire burned higher and higher.

We must try to let Jesus' spirit fill us by reading his words and examples over and over, meditating on them over and over. They should do in our souls what the drop of water does when it falls again and again on the paving stone, always at the same place.[2]

Receive the Gospel. It is by the Gospel, according to the Gospel, that we will be judged. It is not by the book of some spiritual guide or some learned scholar or some saint but by the Gospel of Jesus, the words of Jesus, the examples of Jesus, the counsels of Jesus, the teachings of Jesus.[3]

To Charles the Eucharist meant that Jesus was very close, really very present.

Jesus, my Lord, you are in the Holy Eucharist. You are here, a meter away from me, in this tabernacle. How close by you are, my God, my Savior, my Jesus, my Brother.[4]

He wanted this presence to take possession of him:

> My God, grant me a continual awareness of your presence. And grant me that awed love that we feel in the presence of the one we love passionately and that makes us stay by the beloved person without being able to take our eyes away.[5]

In fact, his adoration was often a matter of staying there in faith even though his prayer was arid and unrewarding:

> When I'm in front of the Blessed Sacrament I have a hard time staying there to pray for very long. I'm in a strange state. Everything seems empty and hollow to me, worthless and without point, except for staying at Our Lord's feet and looking at him. And then when I go to his feet, I'm dry as a bone, without a word or a thought in my head, and often, sad to say, I end up going to sleep. I reason myself into reading, but the whole thing seems empty to me.[6]

The depth of his faith saved him from the risks of an individualistic piety. The Eucharist for him meant Jesus offering his life in intercession for all people, and to love Jesus meant participation in Jesus' self-giving love.

Ever fascinated by the mystery of the Incarnation, he meditated on its implications for the believer: the requirement to love one another.

> See in the Incarnation love for all people, the love God has for them. Therefore you must love them after his example, to be perfect just as your heavenly Father is perfect. This love is active and alive. It is deep. It made God cover at a single leap the distance that separates the finite from the infinite. It made him choose an unprecedented means for our salvation, the Incarnation. God himself came to live on the earth.[7]

While meditating on the Visitation, he caught a glimpse of the apostolic dimension of the life of Nazareth:

> I had hardly taken flesh when I asked my Mother to carry me to the house where John was to be born. Before I was even born myself, I was at work on the sanctification of the human race, and I prompted my Mother to work with me.
>
> And to all the other people to whom I give myself I say: Work with me as my Mother did, without words, in silence, in the midst of people who do not know me. Carry me among them by setting up an altar there, a tabernacle. Take the Gospel there not by preaching it with your lips, but preaching it with your example, not by proclaiming it but by living it.[8]

> Our whole existence, our whole being, should cry the Gospel from the rooftops. Our whole personality should spell Jesus; all our acts, all our life should proclaim that we belong to Jesus and show a mirror of Gospel life.[9]

Thus for Brother Charles his years at Nazareth were a time of desert, when "God spoke to his heart" and when his desire grew deeper:

> What I'm secretly dreaming of, without admitting it to myself, what I can't help dreaming of, is something very simple, for just a few people. It would be like those communities in the early Church. A few people gathered together to lead the life of Nazareth, to live by their work the way the Holy Family did, and practice the Nazareth virtues as they contemplate Jesus.[10]

But the desert also brought trial and temptation. And Brother Charles often doubted his choice as he sought his path during those three years. We see that from his letters to Fr. Huvelin.

For several months he wondered if he ought to go back to the Trappists:

> Sometimes I tell myself I could have done some good if I had stayed with the Trappists, that I would have been superior in two years, and with God's help I could have done some good in that little monastery at Akbes.[11]

The abbess of the Poor Clares in Jerusalem, who had realized their hired man's identity, already pictured him chaplain of the convent and tried to convince him to become a priest, all the while encouraging him to plan how to found his own congregation.

At one moment, when he saw the distress of a poor widow, he did think of "selling himself" as a nurse with the Sisters of Charity to pay the widow's keep.

About that same time he heard of some property for sale at the top of the Mount of the Beatitudes. The idea infatuated him and made him dream of founding a group of priest-hermits there.

> The result of my Holy Week was that I decided to leave Saint Clare's convent. I'm "as pampered as a prize pup" here, if you'll excuse the expression. I wanted to set myself up as a hermit in a vacant spot somewhere in the hills overlooking Nazareth and bear the cross of Jesus there in a life of poverty and work. I had never thought a moment about the Mount of the Beatitudes nor about becoming a priest. But suddenly here I am with the three things at once, fitting together and presenting themselves to me almost under the form of a logical conclusion.[12]

The more I think about it, the more I find it a necessity to be ordained "for the service of holy poverty" — that is, ordained as a hermit. This means being ordained by a bishop who would give tentative approval to a rule I've been following for a year and a half and that I've been thinking about for a long, long, time. This spring it will be seven years since I wrote you from Akbes with the outlines of my project: to lead the life of Our Lady in the mystery of her Visitation, along with a few companions. That is, to sanctify the unbelievers of mission countries. Silently, without preaching, we would bring Jesus in the Blessed Sacrament and the practice of the evangelical virtues into their midst.[13]

Fr. Huvelin, weary of all these ideas for projects, was far from enthusiastic: "Your projects frighten me. I do not think that this idea of priest-hermits comes from God. Still, if you feel irresistibly drawn to it, take your rule, go to the Patriarch of Jerusalem, throw yourself at his feet and ask him for light. For my part, my child, I am in the dark. I see nothing but objections, and I fear a spirit of self-seeking underneath your devotion and your piety."[14]

Brother Charles got no encouragement from the Patriarch, and so he gave up all his projects and returned peacefully to Nazareth.

And then Fr. Huvelin perceived that through all this casting about for a path something had become ripe, and he wrote: "Now I think that it may work. I think you will go towards the Lord and will lead others there and are learning to live the Gospel. I know the Master was guiding it all. It was not that you had to make an idea succeed, it was the will of God you had to find. You had to leave it to grow of itself, gently, peacefully, in littleness and utter lowliness, like Jesus at his beginnings in Bethlehem and during the long incubation at Nazareth."[15]

Take the Banquet to the Poor

On 16 August 1900, Brother Charles returned to France to prepare himself for the priesthood. He spent several months at Our Lady of the Snows.

Before his ordination he made a "retreat of election."[16] He centered it on three of Jesus' sayings that he held especially dear:

> "Into your hands I commit my spirit."
> "He came to bring fire to the earth."
> "He came to seek out and save what was lost."

And his future began to clear. He would not go back to Nazareth:

> It is not where the ground is most hallowed that I must go, but where the souls are in the greatest need.[17]

> My retreats before being ordained to the diaconate and to the priesthood showed me that I ought to lead the life of Nazareth, which is my vocation, not in the Holy Land I love so well but among the people whose souls were most sick, the sheep who were most forsaken. I am the minister of a divine banquet which should be offered not to our brothers, relatives and rich neighbors, but to the crippled and the blind, to the most forsaken souls, where priests are most in shortage.
>
> When I was young I had traveled through Algeria and Morocco. Morocco, as big as France and with a population of ten million people, did not have a single priest away from the coastal areas. In the Algerian Sahara, 7 or 8 times as big as France and more densely populated than used to be thought, there were a dozen missionaries. No people seemed to me more forsaken than these. And so I

sought and obtained permission from the Apostolic Prefect of the Sahara to settle in the Algerian Sahara.[18]

On 9 June 1901, Charles was ordained a priest. On the 23rd he was already writing to his friend H. de Castries, who knew the Sahara well, to ask his advice about where to settle. He explained what he wanted:

> To start a house on the Moroccan border, not a Trappist monastery, not a big and wealthy convent or a farming enterprise, but a sort of humble little hermitage where several poor monks could live from a few fruit trees and a little barley they harvest themselves. They would live strictly cloistered, in penitence and adoration of the Blessed Sacrament, and not go out of their enclosure or preach but offer hospitality to all who come, good or bad, friend or foe, Muslim or Christian.
>
> This would be evangelization not by the word but by the presence of the Blessed Sacrament, the offering of the holy sacrifice, prayer, penitence, the practice of the evangelical virtues, and charity, a brotherly charity offered to all. We would share our bread to the last mouthful with the poor, with our guests, with strangers, and receive any person as our beloved brother or sister.[19]

The Word of God taken seriously is dangerous.

On the threshold of this new step, Brother Charles felt within him the fire that burned the prophet Jeremiah, the fire Jesus came to bring on earth. Like Elijah after the vision on Horeb, God had sent him back to the streets of the world, where people struggle, where Jesus continues to suffer and die, where the poor and the outcast are waiting for the good news.

Charles did not suspect that in letting himself be guided by the logic of the Incarnation he would blaze new trails for the way of contemplation. His inspiration to return to what he had left was the love of his beloved Jesus, the desire to be with him and walk with him where he had met him, "on the streets of Nazareth," as a poor, obscure man in the crowd.

His time at Nazareth had been marked by long contemplation of the Eucharist. Now this would blossom into a Eucharistic life, in which Brother Charles discovered more and more that communion in the Body and Blood of Christ destined him to become, like Christ, a man devoured.

He rediscovered what Saint John Chrysostom had long ago affirmed: "The sacrament of the altar is not to be separated from the sacrament of the neighbor."

God's startling choice of the dispossessed showed Brother Charles what he hadn't seen before. It led him into a life just as contemplative, but one mingled with others and more and more under the sign of hospitality, service, and brotherly sharing with the poorest.

At Beni Abbès, the Algerian oasis closest to the Moroccan border, Brother Charles built his hermitage:

> Not far from the fort and the oasis, yet in a solitary place, I've found a little hollow which is arid but irrigable (water is abundant at Beni Abbès). With the help of God I'm going to make it into a garden, and on the flank of the hill men from the garrison and the Arab Bureau have started building me a dwelling. I am deeply grateful for their kindness and charity. They are using mud bricks and palm trunks and making a chapel, three cells and a guest room. I will move in tomorrow. That's how fast they've been working.[20]

"Whatever You Do to the Least of These"

Charles drew up a precise set of rules for himself as a monk. He even marked off his enclosure with a line of small stones. He decreed he would cross the line only in case of necessity, but he never built a wall and he always left his door open.

> I want all the people here, be they Christians, Muslims, Jews or whatever, to see me as their brother, a universal brother. They have started calling my house "the fraternity" and that gives me pleasure.[21]

Receiving guests would quickly disrupt his way of life:

> Guests, poor people, slaves, visitors — they don't leave me a minute's peace. I'm the only one, with all the work of the monastery to do. I finished the little guest house on the 15th and since then every day we've had guests to lodge and to feed morning and evening. The place hasn't been empty once. There are as many as eleven a night, not counting an old cripple who lives there permanently. I have 60 to 100 visitors a day, quite often if not always.[22]

> It's the same thing every day, poor people, sick people, one after the other. I reproach myself interiorly for not spending enough time in prayer and purely spiritual things. By day people never stop knocking at my door, and at night when it would be a good time for it I fall asleep like a wretch. It shames me and saddens me that sleep takes up more room than I want it to. I haven't time for it and it takes its own.[23]

Attentive to whatever people might need, he let soldiers posted at Beni Abbès come for prayer and the sacraments. They had no other spiritual assistance.

> The willingness of the soldiers around me, and a piety I never hoped to find in them, allow me to hold benediction of the Blessed Sacrament every evening without exception. I precede it with a reading from the Holy

Gospel and a short explanation: I can't get over it that they want to listen to me. After benediction I lead a short prayer.[24]

With surprise I'm seeing myself pass from the contemplative life to a life of ministry. I've been led to it in spite of myself by people's needs.[25]

But the ones farthest away were the ones he wanted to be close to:

Occupy myself especially with the lost sheep, the sinners, the wicked. Mustn't leave the 99 sheep who have gone astray to stay serenely in the fold with the one faithful sheep. Conquer the natural severity I feel towards sinners and replace it with compassion, interest, zeal, diligent care.[26]

He bought freedom for some slaves and baptized a four-year-old child and an old woman. He began dreaming about the birth of a little Christian community.

Pray for my four children in Beni Abbès: Abd-Jesu, who has stayed with me and is becoming more and more of a dear, Paul, Pierre, and Marie. These are the feeble little beginnings of Christianity in these parts.[27]

But he was aware how uncertain the enterprise was, and knew he had to leave things up to God:

Our little beginnings of Christianity here at Beni Abbès seem to be going back down to zero. May the will of Jesus be done. Paul left me in a rather painful way, and Pierre, whose parents live ten days' walk or so from here, wants to go back to them. Marie is going to have her cataracts operated on and if it works she won't have any more reason to stay and can go back to living on her own. There'll be only Abd-Jesu left. He's becoming more of a dear every day and I'm eager to see him in better hands than mine, with the Sisters of Vincent de Paul.[28]

He took these tasks on because he was the only priest for hundreds of kilometers. But he didn't want it to lead him to any other kind of life than the imitation of Jesus at Nazareth, his chosen vocation. After a visit from his bishop, he wrote:

> Bishop Guérin seems to have a little, discrete tendency to push me gently towards transforming my life as a silent and hidden monk, my life of Nazareth, into life as a missionary. This tendency I shall not follow, for I believe I would be very unfaithful to God, who gave me a vocation to the hidden and silent life and not to the life of a man of words. Both monks and missionaries are apostles, but in different ways. On this point I shall not yield, and I'll keep following the path that I've lived well or poorly for 14 years, most often poorly, sad to say, but faithfully. I'll live Jesus' hidden life with others if Jesus sends them, alone if he leaves me alone.[29]

By receiving the poorest, he discovered the conditions they lived in, and he was not slow to realize concretely how extremely oppressed they were.

> I had believed and I had heard that slavery among the Muslims was a rather lenient affair. Now that I speak to many slaves a day on familiar terms, and particularly when I speak to them out of hearing of their masters, I can see how wrong I was. They are overworked (getting water for the palm plantations), beaten daily, underfed and underclothed, and if they try to run away — which happens frequently — there is an armed pursuit.[30]

Charles, a product of his times, did not call colonialism as such into question. But every time he witnessed flagrant injustices he took a forceful stand against them.

In front of the "abomination of slavery" he tried to do what he could. He kept his door open to the hungry. Beyond this, he managed to redeem a few young slaves and return them to freedom. When he realized that the French authorities tacitly complied with such an "abomination," he looked for a way to rouse public opinion. Throughout 1902, he wrote letter after letter.

To Dom Martin, the Abbot of Our Lady of the Snows, he expressed his indignation:

> What you say is what I am doing concerning the slaves. But having said it, and giving them all the relief I can, I do not think my duty is over. I have to say, or get the appropriate people to say, "This is not allowed. Woe to you hypocrites," who print on your stamps and all around, Liberty, Equality, Fraternity, Human Rights, while you fasten slaves in irons. You throw into the dungeon those who counterfeit your banknotes while you allow children to be stolen from their parents and publicly sold. You punish the theft of a chicken while you permit the theft of a man. (In fact, almost all the slaves of this region were born free and kidnapped from their parents as children.)
>
> Next, we must love our neighbor as ourselves and treat these poor people as we would like to be treated. We must keep any of those God has entrusted to us from being lost, and he entrusts to us all the people in our territory.
>
> It's not for us to get involved in worldly government, no one is more convinced of that than I am. But we must love justice and hate evil, and when the worldly government commits a deep injustice towards those who are in some way under our care (I am the only priest in this

prefecture for 300 km in any direction), we must tell them so. For we are the ones who on earth represent justice and truth, and we do not have the right to be "sleeping sentinels" and "dumb watchdogs" and "useless shepherds." [Is 56:9–11, see Ez 34]

In a word, I'm wondering if (presuming we completely agree about what should be done towards the slaves) we mustn't speak out directly or indirectly to make this injustice known in France. Slavery is a sanctioned theft going on in our regions, and we must say or get someone to say, "Look what is happening. This is not allowed."

I have notified the Apostolic Prefect, maybe that's enough. Far be it from me to want to speak and write, but I do not want to betray my children or fail to do for Jesus, living in his members, what he needs. It is Jesus caught in this wretched situation: "Whatever you did to the least of these, you did to me." I don't want to be a bad shepherd or a dumb watchdog. I'm afraid I might sacrifice Jesus for my peace and the quiet I'm so fond of, or for my cowardice and natural timidity.[31]

He set out the problem in detail for his bishop and begged him to intervene. He asked his advice on what to do:

The biggest question is slavery. One of my friends offered me a chance to put the matter into the hands of Baron Cochin, a fervent anti-slavery campaigner in the Chamber of Deputies. I did not accept for the moment, as I wanted to leave it up to you. But might you not be able to see M. Cochin when you go to France soon?

Going into long detail on the mistreatment inflicted on the slaves in the Saoura region and its oases seems the wrong approach to me. True, they are mistreated, but whether they are treated better or worse, the great injustice is that they are slaves!

Slavery is all the more unjust here. (It is always unjust

for we are all children of Adam and commanded to "treat others as you would like them to treat you.") But besides the huge and monstrous injustice that is always at the root of slavery, there is a special injustice here: very few of the slaves are children of slaves. Almost all of them were kidnapped as children, either from the Sudan or from Touat, when they were 5 years old, or 10 or 15.

My beloved Father, I think the words of Jesus are an obligation on me: "Treat others as you would like them to treat you." I must do what I can for these poor people who are my children and who are yours even more so.[32]

Bishop Guérin, clearly horrified by Brother Charles' proposals, explained to him they were out of place. "As for the slavery question, my very dear father, what can I say to you? More than on any other point I feel myself led to tell you: beware of your own zeal. Be very prudent, lay the sorrow you feel at the feet of Jesus. Beware of getting carried away by your zeal into active intervention. Slavery, there is no doubting it, is a social evil we cannot deplore enough, and Jesus' charity can never fill us too much. But to fight slavery, we must take into account the circumstances of the people we live among. We don't want to lose what means we may have for doing a little good by firing off bombshells which will bring no results besides. This is Archbishop Livinhac's private opinion. A public denunciation at present of what is going on in the South would only make it that much harder to do what we're now doing for people."[33]

Brother Charles submitted, but not without saying that the reasons given hadn't convinced him:

I will obey to the letter the line of conduct you've given me. The reasons you have been good enough to express to me with such affection and which have weight in that they come from you and from Archbishop Livinhac, do not leave me without regrets. Let me say it one last time, since a childlike soul should have no secrets from its Father and let everything come out without holding anything back inside, I regret that the representatives of Jesus content themselves with defending this cause "in whispers" (and not "from the rooftops"), for it is the cause of justice and charity.[34]

To Dom Martin he had written:

Where I fail to agree with you is that I find you much too easily accept evil and try to make the best of it.[35]

Brother Charles felt strongly that in such situations charity does not consist only of relieving suffering. When oppressive structures are intrinsically evil, you must go to the root of the evil and get rid of them.

The current regime must end and slavery must be abolished. Justice and right require it.[36]

No human power has the right to keep these wretched people in irons whom God created as free as we are. And if we allow their so-called masters to hold onto them by force and pursue them when they try to escape, if we give them back to their masters when they ask the French authorities for asylum, having hoped in vain to find protection and justice there, then we are robbing them of their most undeniable rights.[37]

When Brother Charles reacted against injustice, he always did so motivated by the Word of God, the Gospel taken literally. He realized there more forcefully the concrete solidarity with the poorest that Jesus' words commit us to: "What you did to one of the least of these brothers or sisters of mine, you did to me":

"I was hungry, I was thirsty, I was a stranger, I was naked, sick, in prison, and you never helped, welcomed, visited me. Whatever you did not do to the least of these, you did not do it to me." [Mt 25:42–45]

What a weighty saying. It is not there for us to make up commentaries about but to believe. We must see clearly that what we could have done for someone and did not do, it is Our Lord we have neglected to do it for.

He did not say all the good we refused to do, no, all the good we did not do, all we could have done and neglected to do. The passerby who is poor, naked, a stranger, in trouble, asks nothing from us, but that person is a member of Jesus, a part of Jesus, a portion of Jesus. We let the person go by us and give him none of what he needs: it is Jesus we have let go by.

This emphatically means we owe ourselves to our neighbors, body and soul. We owe our neighbors our hearts and our minds. This is what the example of Our Lord should say to us when he sums up his life in a single sentence: "The Son of Man came to serve and to give his life as a ransom for many."[38]

A few months before his death, Brother Charles wrote to his friend Louis Massignon:

I think there is no saying in the Gospel that made a deeper impression on me and more transformed my life than this one: "Whatever you did to one of the least of these you did it to me."

If we remember that these are the words of Uncreated Truth and come from the same lips that said, "This is my Body, this is my Blood," how compellingly we are moved to seek out Jesus and love him in the "least ones," the sinners, the poor.[39]

Brother Charles' conviction that Jesus is just as really present in any person suffering poverty and oppression as he is in the Eucharist not only transformed his life but unified it as well. The same love that compelled him to spend hours before the Blessed Sacrament incited him to commit himself to the liberation of the slaves in whom he saw Jesus suffering and dying.

A Brother's Presence
at the Heart of the Desert

The Call of the Hoggar: Move on Again?

When he had chosen Beni Abbès, Brother Charles had gone as far away as he could go. But now a way into the South was opening up, a road into Tuareg country, to the Hoggar.

In June 1903 his friend Laperrine wrote to him about it at length. Among other things, he told Charles about the remarkable actions of a Tuareg woman during a battle between some Tuaregs and some French soldiers. Her name was Tarichat Oult Ibdakane. "She stood up against the tribesmen who wished to finish off the wounded; instead, she took them home and cared for them. When Attisi came back wounded from the fight and wanted to execute the wounded prisoners himself, she wouldn't let him into her house. When the soldiers had recovered, she got them back to Tripoli."[1]

Brother Charles found her actions admirable and straight away composed in his journal a letter he wanted his bishop to write to this woman:

> The first commandment of religion is to love God with all our heart. The second is to love all people without exception, as we love ourselves. With admiration and thanksgiving to God to see how well you practice love towards your fellow human beings, we write you this letter. We want you to know that among Christians, all the religious people who will hear about you will bless you and praise God for your virtues. They will ask God to grant you all blessings in this world and give you glory in heaven. We are also writing to ask you earnestly to pray for us, for we are convinced that God, who has put into your heart a will to love him and serve him, will hear the prayers you send up to him.[2]

From then on Brother Charles began to feel a call to go to the Hoggar. He knew that he could join a military convoy to that region that his friend Laperrine was organizing. He began debating and struggling with himself about it.

> My nature recoils from it exceedingly. I shudder — and am ashamed of it — at the thought of leaving Beni Abbès, where it is so calm at the foot of the altar, and throwing myself into traveling. I dread traveling enormously now. My reason too comes up with drawbacks to the idea. Am I to leave the tabernacle at Beni Abbès empty, go away from this place where there just might be fighting (though not very likely), and waste my energies in these travels, which are no good for the soul? Would I not glorify God more by adoring him in solitude? Aren't solitude and the life of Nazareth my vocation?
> After reason has said all that, I see before me those vast regions without a priest. I see myself the only priest able

to go there, and more and more intensely I feel an urge to go. I'd like to go at least once. According to how it turns out, according to what the experience shows me, I'll decide whether to go back again or not. In spite of what my reason tells me and my nature's dread of being away from here, more and more I feel inside myself a strong urge to make this trip.[3]

Thus by his deepest inner feelings, where his desires most match the desires of Jesus, Brother Charles discerns the will of God. The sign is his inward urge, stronger than all the arguments of his reason.

He still had the same single-minded passion: to let Jesus lead him, fill him and transform him by his words and examples. We can see Charles becoming freer and more malleable in God's hands.

There's just one item of good I see in myself: it's my constant will to do what pleases God most, always and in everything. But as for carrying it out, what a lot of falls.[4]

Initially his bishop hesitated, but finally gave permission. After a four-month-long exhausting trek through the desert, in May of 1904 Brother Charles arrived in the Hoggar. The place captivated him immediately.

He wrote to Fr. Huvelin:

I'm living from one day to the next. As long as I can usefully stay in this country and others haven't come to replace me, I shall stay here. There needs to be somebody at a post like this.

At the moment I'm a tent-dwelling nomad, changing places constantly. It's a good thing for the beginnings, for it lets me meet a lot of people and see a lot of regions, but as soon as I can settle down and stay somewhere permanently, I shall.[5]

He had taken a new step. More than ever he based his attitude toward his situation upon his insights into Jesus of Nazareth. He did not seek a solitary place to build his hermitage, but one accessible to everybody:

> It is love which must focus your life of prayer, not distance from my children. See me in them. And as I did at Nazareth, live beside them, rapt in God.[6]

Looking back on what he had been doing up till then, he sought an approach humbler and more unobtrusive than the one he had taken at Beni Abbès:

> Lead the life of Jesus at Nazareth by the rule of the Little Brothers of the Sacred Heart. Be as little and as poor as Jesus was at Nazareth. Not try, as I did at Beni Abbès, to get a nest ready for my companions. God will give the nest if he sends the souls. Not try, as I did at Beni Abbès, to give away a lot in alms. If I have anything over, just give that. That was how Jesus, Mary and Joseph did it at Nazareth. Not try on my own to provide alms and hospitality as a fraternity of 25 Little Brothers would be able to do it. When in doubt, always do as Jesus did at Nazareth.[7]

The following year he returned to the trails of the Hoggar:

> In everything and for everything, take the life of Nazareth as my object, whether alone or with a few brothers, until such time as it becomes really possible to lead a life completely as Little Brothers and Little Sisters in a cloistered Nazareth. Let Nazareth be my model, in all its simplicity and breadth, using my rule as a handbook of guidelines which will sometimes help me find the way to the life of Nazareth.
>
> For example, until the Little Brothers and Little Sisters are duly established, no habit, like Jesus at Nazareth. No

cloister, like Jesus at Nazareth. No withdrawn, out-of-the-way habitations, but a house near a village, like Jesus at Nazareth. No less than 8 hours of work a day (manual or other sorts, but manual as much as possible), like Jesus at Nazareth.[8]

And in his diary for 11 August 1905, he wrote:

I have the possibility of settling down to live at Tamanrasset or anywhere else in the Hoggar. I could have a house and a garden and settle down there for good. This possibility even seems to me like my Beloved's will.

I choose Tamanrasset, a village of twenty households right in the mountains, in the heart of the Hoggar and the Dag Rali, who are its principal tribe. It is far from any of the important centers. It's unlikely it will ever have a garrison, telegraph lines or a European presence, and there will not be a mission here for a long time. I'm choosing this forsaken spot and I'm settling here, imploring Jesus to bless this endeavor where I want my life to have as its sole model his life at Nazareth.

May he in his love deign to convert me, make me the way he wants me to be, make me love him with all my heart. Let me love him, obey him and imitate him as much as I can at every instant of my life. Sacred Heart of Jesus, your Kingdom come.[9]

To his cousin Marie, he provided details on the construction of his hermitage and about his projects:

My house is getting built: two rooms, each 1.75 meters wide and 2.75 long, about 2 meters high. The walls are earth and stone. It will be finished in 5 or 6 days. Afterwards we'll build a reed hut to use as parlor, dining room, kitchen, bedroom for Paul, guest rooms. For the security of the Blessed Sacrament, I'll sleep beside it.

> I picture myself leading the life of Nazareth here for an indefinite time. Paul will work in the garden with me and I'll make wooden platters. I'll try to do a little good to the people around me and pray to our one Beloved.[10]

As soon as he had come into contact with the Tuaregs in their country, he had started studying their language and undertaken to compile a dictionary. He was also preparing a translation of the Gospels and some passages from the Wisdom Books of the Old Testament that seemed especially appropriate.

> The time I don't spend walking or resting I use to prepare the ways. I try to make friends with the Tuaregs, and I make lexicons and translations that those who come here to bring Jesus will absolutely need.[11]

> I divide my time between prayer, relations with the local people and my work on the Tuareg language. I give this last thing a big place. First, I'd like to get it over and done with and be altogether free for the other things. And besides, I need this language work. I can't do the Tuaregs any good except by speaking with them and knowing their language.[12]

In fact, the language was not all that Brother Charles studied. He took an interest in the people's culture and started paying attention to all its elements. Over the years he transcribed the poems people sang in the evening around the fire, lyrics which transmitted the tribe's history and soul. Three days before his death he noted: "finished the translation of the collection of Tuareg poems."

Approachable and Unimposing

Remaining by himself in the Hoggar meant, by the liturgical rules of the times, that Brother Charles had to give up celebrating the Eucharist as long as there were no other Christians with him. His bishop asked him about this and he answered:

> You ask me if it's better to live in the Hoggar without being able to celebrate the Holy Mass or to celebrate Mass but not live there. I've often asked myself the same thing. I used to incline always to sacrifice everything else to the celebration of Holy Mass. But there must be something wrong with this line of reasoning. Since the Apostles, the greatest saints have sometimes sacrificed their possibility of celebrating Mass to works of spiritual charity.
>
> Living alone in a place is a good thing. You achieve something even if you don't do much, because you start to belong to the country. You're approachable and unimposing there: it gives you such "littleness."[13]

This is not to say that his choice didn't cost him deeply. Besides, adaptation was hard. Brother Charles suffered from isolation and went through a period of depression. Prayer had become a real struggle:

> I'm not pleased with myself. I'm lax and cold. My prayers are extremely lukewarm, I've no mortification, my life is banal, passionless and empty. Prayer is difficult for me. As soon as I start, I'm attacked by sleep or by unbearable thoughts. This difficulty comes no matter what time I try to pray.
>
> Am I wrong to distract myself like this? Would it be better to go on with my exercises of piety and not cut a minute off them, just asking God to help me?[14]

He had hopes of getting a companion in 1907, but the man fell sick and had to turn around before he even got to the Hoggar.

To him, his life seemed like a failure:

> You know my wretchedness. You know how much I need you to pray for me. Over 21 years ago you brought me back to Jesus. What a harvest I should have by now, for myself and for others. And instead of that, I have wretchedness and bankruptcy for myself, and not the least good for others. A tree can be told by its fruits, and mine show what I am.[15]

A terrible drought held the Hoggar in its grip:

> This year has been hard for the country. It hasn't rained for 17 months. That means raging famine in a country that lives on its milk, and where the poor have almost nothing else than milk to live on. The goats are as dry as the earth is, and the people as dry as the goats.[16]

He shared his reserves to the bottom of his stock. Finally he reached a state of exhaustion himself, and after one Christmas when he had felt himself very alone he fell sick.

> Christmas. No Mass tonight, for the first Christmas in 21 years. May my Beloved's will be done. In his mercy he's still let me have the Blessed Sacrament here. Up till the last minute I had hoped that someone would come, but nothing happened. No Christian traveler or soldier came, and I didn't get my permission to celebrate Mass alone. It's been three months, more than three months since I got any letters.[17]

> I've been rather sick these past days. I don't know just what it is, something wrong with my heart, I think. I'm not coughing, no chest pains, but the slightest movement

leaves me so out of breath I could almost faint. A day or two ago I thought I might be going to die.[18]

This time, in his state of debility and sickness, he was the one who was poor. Up until then he had been trying to be approachable and unimposing, but he was still the one doing the giving, aiding others when they were in distress. Now he was the one who needed them, and it was the Tuaregs who would save him, giving him their most precious possession in that time of famine:

> The people went around to all the goats for a radius of 4 km to get me a little milk.[19]

Only when he had been reduced to a state of extreme need, were the Tuaregs able to give him something. The reversal in their situations provided the ground from which genuine friendships could spring up and grow between Brother Charles and the Tuaregs. Friendship needs reciprocity and sharing.

> The Tuaregs around here treat me with growing trust. Those I was already friends with are now closer, and new friendships are forming. I do them what services I can. I try to show them my love. When it seems like a favorable occasion, I speak about natural religion, about God's commandments, his Love, how to live in harmony with his Will, loving one's neighbor, and so on.[20]

The Apostolate of Friendship

In 1909, he wrote:

> My apostolate should be one of goodness. When people see me they should say: "If this man is good, his religion must be good."

> If someone asks me why I am mild and good, I should say: "Because I am the servant of someone much better than I am. If you only knew how good my master Jesus is." I want to be good enough that people will say: "If this is what the servant is like, what must the master be?"[21]

At a time when people often claimed simplistically, "Outside the Church, no salvation," he confided to a Protestant friend:

> I am not here to convert the Tuaregs all at once, but to try to understand them. I am sure that God will welcome those who have been good and upright into heaven. You are a Protestant, T. is an agnostic, the Tuaregs are Muslims. I'm convinced that God will receive us all if we have deserved it.[22]

Since reaching the Hoggar, he had always known that there was no question of looking for converts:

> I'm not to talk to them directly about Our Lord. That would just make them go away. I'm to gain their confidence, make friends with them, do them little services, deepen a friendship between us and encourage them discreetly to abide by natural religion.[23]

But deep in his heart he kept a boundless desire that the people might one day know that God was their Father and that Jesus had died for them:

> Will it be given to the generations that come after us to see the multitudes of North Africa say together, "Our Father who are in Heaven, hallowed be your name, your kingdom come, your will be done on earth as in heaven," and address God as the Father of all humanity, knowing that they are all brothers and sisters in him, loving their neighbors as themselves? I do not know. It is the secret of

God. But it is our duty to work towards it with all our strength. It is an application of the second commandment to love our neighbors as ourselves, so like the first commandment, to love God above all else.[24]

In 1910, he started building a second hermitage up in the mountains on the Assekrem plateau about 60 kilometers from Tamanrasset:

> I don't see many Tuaregs just now. They are all up in the mountains, in the area of the spot where I'm having my hermitage built and where in the future, I'll spend half the time I consecrate to the Tuaregs. Construction started on the hermitage a month ago and it should be finished by now. It's right in the heart of the Hoggar, in the most central point of the mountain range which forms the people's citadel. Their tents (that is, their women, children, and old people) always stay within it.[25]

He spent several months there in 1911. The beauty of the panorama moved him:

> The view is more beautiful than anyone can express or even imagine. Nothing can give you an idea of the forest of peaks and rocky spires I have at my feet. It is a marvel. You cannot see it without thinking of God. I have a hard time taking my eyes away from this wonderful view. The beauty of it and the impression of infinity it gives you bring you close to the Creator.[26]

But the possibility of deepened contacts with the Tuaregs made him happiest:

> I'm very pleased with my stay here. People come to see me every 4 or 5 days at least, even though the camps are far from here at the moment because of the drought. Since my visitors come from a day, a day and a half, or

two days away, they finish the day with me and sleep here. A meal or two in common, a day or a day and a half spent together, draw you closer than a large number of visits a half-hour or an hour long, as they are at Tamanrasset.[27]

The years passed and Brother Charles became more and more involved in every aspect of the life of his Tuareg friends. In many little ways he sought to better their living conditions. During his last visit to France he asked his cousin to teach him to knit, and on 16 April 1915 he wrote to her:

> The knitting and crocheting have worked out well. The women are learning both and quite a few young people are crocheting sweaters. We have run out of hooks and yarn. If you could send some of both and also send some cottonseed by Vilmorin you would be doing a great service for the country. These things are also useful spiritually because everything is connected. It is easier for them to understand material progress and through working concretely for it they become used to work. This in turn will help them have a more settled life, open their minds to other ways and make them desirous of wider travel. Materially they have already made great progress. When I first arrived here there were two tiny houses and fifty huts. Now there are eighty houses, including one very sturdy one with a hut attached. And it is thus in all areas of life....[28]

Already in Nazareth Brother Charles had written a meditation on the words of Jesus after the raising of Jairus' daughter, "Give her something to eat":

> Have that tender care that expresses itself in the little things that are like a balm for the heart.... With our

neighbors go into the smallest details, whether it is a question of health, of consolation, of prayerfulness, or of need. Console and ease the pain of others through the tiniest of attentions. Be as tender and attentive towards those whom God puts on our path, as a brother towards brother or as a mother for her child. As much as possible be an element of consolation for those around us, as soothing balm, as our Lord was towards all those who drew near to him.

He had written to Bishop Guérin: "For the spreading of the Gospel I am ready to go to the end of the world and live till the last judgment."[29] The same desire that made him write now burned higher and higher. Facing such an immense task, he was still alone. At that point he foresaw with amazing intuition the importance of lay people for evangelization. This triggered his final project: an association of lay people, the Union of Brothers and Sisters of the Sacred Heart of Jesus.

Writing to one of the first members of this association, J. Hours, Charles set out the fundamental nature and principles of such evangelization. In this important letter, Brother Charles vigorously summed up his deepest conception of the meaning of mission, as the Gospel and his own experience gave him light to see it:

> I have received your letter. You say things that are quite true about the need everywhere, in France as in mission countries, for the work of the Church to be backed up by the work of lay people. I have been thinking along these same lines for some time.
>
> As you say, the ecclesiastical world and the world of lay people have so little to do with each other that the clergy give the laity no chance. It is certain that working

alongside priests there need to be Priscillas and Aquilas [see Acts 18:2, 18–19], who can see what the priest does not see, go where the priest cannot go. They can reach those who escape the priest and evangelize them by a contact that does them good, by a kindness that over-flows to all, a love always ready to give itself, a good example attracting those who turn their backs on the priest and are determined to be hostile to him.

I think the problem goes very deep. Basic virtues are missing, or else are not strong enough. Virtues funda-mental to Christian life — like charity, humility, mild-ness — are shallow and misunderstood.

Charity, which is the heart of religion (our first duty is to love God; our second, which is like the first, is to love our neighbor as ourselves) obliges all Christians to love their neighbor, meaning every human being, as them-selves and consequently to make their neighbor's salva-tion, like their own, the great aim of their lives.

Every Christian must therefore be an apostle. This is not a counsel, it is a commandment, the commandment of charity.

To be an apostle, how? By the means God puts at each person's disposal. Priests have their superiors who tell them what they should do. Lay people must be apostles towards all those they can reach: their relations and their friends first of all, but not only these. There is nothing narrow about charity. Its scope is as wide as the dimen-sions of the heart of Jesus. How to be an apostle? By the best means available, according to who it is the apostles are trying to reach. With anyone they are in touch with, making no exceptions, they must work by goodness, kindness, friendliness, the example of virtue, by humility and mildness, always such attractive and such Christian attitudes. With some people they should never say a word about God or religion, but wait patiently as God waits patiently, be good as God is good, show respectful affection and pray. With others they should speak of God to the extent that these are ready for it, and as soon as they reach the point of wanting to seek the truth by studying religion, they can put them in touch with a well-chosen priest who will know how to do them good.

Above all, apostles must see every human being as their brother or sister: "You are all brothers and sisters since you have only one Father, and he is in heaven." They must see every human being as a child of God, a soul redeemed by the blood of Jesus, a soul Jesus loves, a soul we must love as we love ourselves and whose salvation we must work for.

We must banish any spirit of triumphalism. "I am sending you out like sheep among wolves," Jesus said. How far from Jesus' way of speaking and acting is the triumphalist spirit of some who are not Christians, or who are bad ones, and who see enemies to combat where they should see ailing brothers and sisters to care for, wounded victims lying on the path for whom they should be good Samaritans.

It would appear that parents in the home, priests at their catechism lessons and all whose mission it is to rear children and train the young, should instill these truths in them from their earliest years and keep coming back to them:

— Every Christian must be an apostle. It is an obligatory duty of charity.

— Every Christian must see each human being as a beloved brother or sister. A sinner, an enemy of God, the Christian must see as someone ill, very ill, and should feel a deep pity and should care for that person as for a wayward brother or sister. Non-Christians may have a Christian for their enemy; the Christian must always be a loving friend towards every person and have towards them all the same feelings as Jesus has in his Heart.

— Be charitable, mild and humble towards all people. This is what Jesus taught us to do. Do not set out to conquer anybody. Jesus taught us to go "like lambs among wolves" and not to speak roughly or spitefully, not to throw insults, not to take up arms.

— Make themselves all things to all people in order to give Jesus to them all. Do it by having kindness and friendliness towards everyone, by rendering them all possible services, by contacts with them that show affection, by caring about them all and treating them as brothers and sisters. And thus, lead souls gradually to Jesus by putting into practice Jesus' goodness.

— Read the Holy Gospels over and over continually in order to have Jesus' actions, words and thoughts constantly in mind. In this way, come to think, speak, and act as Jesus would, and not by the examples and modes of the world, whose practices we quickly fall back into if we take our eyes away from our Divine Model.

This is the remedy, in my opinion. To apply it is difficult because it touches very basic things, the inner realities of the soul, and because the need for it is universal. But difficulty is not there to make us stop trying. The greater the difficulty, the more we must rather set to work rapidly and strive with all our might. God always helps those who want to serve him. Never has God failed his creatures. It is we creatures who fail God so often. Even if we are doomed not to succeed, we should work with no less ardor, for when we work for this cause we are doing nothing else than obeying God and accomplishing his will as he has made it known to us.[30]

In the Likeness of Jesus
Even Unto Death

The Means Jesus Used

As the years went by, Brother Charles could feel his physical strength diminishing. He wrote to his cousin:

> Don't worry. I don't have the strength any more to kill myself working. When I do just a little bit more than my limit, I feel it straight away and I slow down. I put all I can into it, but it's far from being as much as I used to do. Besides, I'm so often interrupted by visits that I have plenty of unplanned relaxations.[1]

He kept on going and felt deep peace about it:

> I cannot say that I desire death. I used to desire it, but now I see so much good to be done, so many souls without a shepherd, that what I most want is to do a little good and work a little for the salvation of those poor souls. Still, God loves them far more than I do and doesn't need me. May his will be done.

There's nothing really wrong with me, but the summer
wears me down. I get feverish spells sometimes, head-
aches, sleepless nights. Nothing that lasts and nothing
severe. It will go away when the hot weather does, in five
weeks. I'm leading my usual life, but getting less work
done.[2]

In this final stage of his life, Brother Charles seems to
have surrendered himself more and more into God's hands:
"His will be done." He made Jesus' prayer at Gethsemane
his own, the prayer of total self-surrender to love:

"We are to love God, then, because he loved us first." [1
Jn 4:19] The Passion on Calvary is a supreme declaration
of love. It was to redeem us that you suffered so much, O
Jesus. The least of your acts has infinite worth, since it is
one of God's acts, and would have been more than ample
enough to redeem a thousand worlds, to redeem all possible worlds. But you suffered so much because you wanted
to make us holy, to bear our burdens and to draw us into
loving you freely. Loving is the most powerful way to
attract love, loving is the most powerful way to make one-
self loved.

It is impossible for us to love him and not imitate him,
to love him and not want to be the way he was, do what
he did, suffer and die in torment because he suffered and
died in torment. It is impossible to love him and want to
be crowned with roses when he was crowned with thorns.
We must love him as he has loved us.[3]

In 1900 Brother Charles had written to Fr. Huvelin from
Nazareth:

My life goes on exactly the same way. It is more and more
secluded and silent, more and more hidden and lost to
view. I am delighted to see myself becoming invisible.[4]

It may be that he still took a little satisfaction in his solitary "seclusion" at Nazareth.

Now Brother Charles was linked by deep bonds to the Tuareg people. He had waited in vain to have followers. He was growing old, and felt like a tree with no fruit. "Unless a wheat grain falls on the ground and dies, it remains only a single grain. But if it dies, it yields a rich harvest." [Jn 12:24]

To be a savior with Jesus, we have to pass as he did through suffering, apparent failure and death:

> The means Jesus used at his birth in the Manger, at Nazareth and on the Cross are these: poverty, utter lowliness, humiliation, rejection, persecution, suffering, the cross. These are the only weapons he has given us to fight with, the ones used by our divine Bridegroom, who asks us to let him continue his life in us. Let us follow him as our sole model and we are sure to do much good, for in that case it will not be we who live but he who lives in us. Our acts will no longer be our own, human and frail, but his divinely efficacious acts.[5]

The War Years

On 3 August 1914, war broke out between France and Germany. A month later, when Brother Charles finally heard about it, the news rocked him. What ought he do?

Soon afterwards, on 15 September, he wrote to his cousin:

> You'll sense how deeply it costs me to be so far from our soldiers and the front. But my duty obviously is to stay here.[6]

However, he was tormented by the thought of his comrades in combat. In December he wrote to his friend, General Laperrine:

> Wouldn't I be more useful at the front as a chaplain or stretcher bearer? If you don't write me to come I will stay here peacefully, but if you say come I will leave immediately and make haste.[7]

Laperrine's answer came two months later: "Stay where you are."

The war moved Charles deeply because it touched his own roots: his memory of the War of 1870, the city he had had to flee, the birthplace he had never seen again.

He wrote to G. Tourdes, his childhood friend:

> My dear Gabriel,
> How I think of you since the war began! How much I thought about you when I heard about the combats at Saint Dié, the city falling and being taken back again. I worry about you, worry about your brother, worry about your nephew who is probably under fire. Please, please, send me news. We'll talk about all the rest when we see each other after the war is won. If, as I firmly hope, we come out the winners, we will make a trip together to visit Strasbourg as a French city again.[8]

Reading these letters and others which contain harsh judgments on the enemy, we feel Charles' whole being vibrating in tune with the wave of patriotism that was sweeping his country. He was a man of his time, rooted in a historical epoch and molded by the human surroundings that produced him. This was the human clay that God had to work with.

Torn two ways by the situation, in spite of everything he chose to stay in the Hoggar, where the repercussions of the conflict soon made themselves felt.

The French army reduced the number of troops stationed in Algeria, and a rebel movement started to develop, supported by Tripolitania (today's Libya) and other foreign powers. Armed raiding parties from Morocco also became more and more of a threat.

Brother Charles, alone at Tamanrasset, was in a very exposed position. The officers of the nearest garrison advised him to come and live there, but he declined. He wanted to stay with the handful of people who in 1905 had allowed him to come and live with them, when others the year before had refused to let him stay.[9]

The passing years had brought deeper familiarity and mutual respect, and friendship had grown. Now, in the hour of his friends' danger, Brother Charles, bonded to them by new solidarity, could not abandon them.

His death would show that human bonds of mutual love are stronger than all the nationalisms that keep us apart.

Moussa Ag Amastan, the Tuareg chieftain who had let Charles stay, wrote to Brother Charles' sister two weeks after Charles' death:

> Much blessing descend on our friend Marie. As soon as I learnt of the death of our friend, your brother Charles, my eyes clouded over. All has become dark for me. I wept and shed many tears and I am in deep mourning. His death gives me greatest sorrow.
>
> ... Greet on my behalf your daughters, your husband and all your friends and say to them: "Charles the Marabout has not died only for you. He has also died for us all. May God grant him mercy and may we all be together with him in Paradise."[10]

To Give One's Life out of Love

Brother Charles had long wanted to die a martyr.

At the monastery of Akbes in 1896, he had witnessed the horrible massacre of the Armenians by the Turks, and had suffered because he felt his nationality was protecting him.

He had written at that time to his cousin:

> All over Armenia, and quite close to us too, there have been terrible massacres. But we were never in any real danger, I think. Because we're Europeans, the Turkish government takes great precautions to keep anything from happening to us. But for the Armenians it was horrible; people speak of 100,000 killed.[11]

> At the end of March, we at Akbes and all the Christians for two days around ought to have been dead. I was not found worthy. That is justified a thousand times, but what a sorrow I feel. Pray for me that I be converted and that God will not refuse me the next time.[12]

Perhaps he was remembering scenes of this massacre when he wrote from Nazareth on 6 June 1897:

> Picture yourself dying a martyr, stripped of everything, stretched out on the ground, naked, unrecognizable, covered with blood and with wounds, violently and painfully slain — and desire it to happen today.[13]

At Beni Abbès he noted:

> Prepare constantly for martyrdom and receive it without a shadow of self-defense, as did the Lamb of God. Receive martyrdom in Jesus, through Jesus, like Jesus and for Jesus.[14]

At Tamanrasset, he wrote again in a prayer:

My Lord Jesus, you said, "There is no greater love than to lay down one's life for one's friends." With all my heart I want to give my life for you, I beg it of you earnestly. Nevertheless, not my will but yours be done. I offer you my life, do with me whatever you want most. My God, forgive my enemies and bring them to salvation.[15]

In 1916, the insecurity worsened. Tamanrasset was threatened both by raiding parties from Morocco and by the Tuareg tribes that had joined the rebellion.

These threats led Brother Charles to develop a new plan. He told Laperrine his reasons for it:

> This is to announce to you my change of residence. I've even moved to a new neighborhood. After living on the left bank of the Wadi Tamanrasset for 11 years in the hermitage you're familiar with, I've shifted to the right bank, on the little plateau on the north side and near the big tree.
>
> Here's why: about a year and a half ago when I could see the Moroccan bandits getting closer and closer to the Hoggar, I thought of building a little refuge here, a tiny Casbah. That way the population of Tamanrasset could take shelter in case the Moroccan raiders came here.
>
> I thought it over and asked the Dag Rali, my neighbors, their opinion. I saw they liked the idea and so I spoke to Saint-Léger and de la Roche about it and then made up my mind. I started building it about a year ago, a very small affair, with just one workman helping me, a Haratin from the village. I picked the place for it with Ouksem. It's approximately on the highest point where the right bank of the riverbed rises up to the plateau, 150 meters from the big tree. It's a square enclosure with a courtyard 14 meters on a side and a turret at each corner. The walls are solid: a meter thick in good solid bricks.
>
> As the construction was progressing, my Tuareg

neighbors talked me into living there. They said that for one thing I would be nearer to them, and that, for another, if ever they had to take refuge, it would be nicer to find someone living there and the place stocked with provisions and tools. I finally let myself be persuaded and put up some rooms on the inside for myself to live in. The space of the courtyard is not significantly reduced and it's still large enough to receive the whole population of the village, including the nearby nomads. I moved in a week ago, even though construction is not quite terminated, because in order to finish it I needed the rafters, doors and windows from my old hermitage.[16]

As we see, Brother Charles made his decision to relocate his hermitage at his neighbors' request, "so that he could be nearer to them."

Some soldiers from the nearest French outpost had stored arms in this refuge. They were to be distributed to thirty or so Tuaregs in charge of protecting Tamanrasset. Were the arms still there on 1 December? This is a disputed question.

Brother Charles' motivation is clear. He had built the "bordj," as his construction was called, to offer shelter to a population of poor and defenseless people with whom he felt solidarity.

There is one case when we must resist evil forcefully. It is when it is not a case of defending ourselves but of protecting others. It takes forcefulness to defend the weak and the innocent when their oppressors wrong them. The spirit of peace is not a spirit of weakness but a spirit of strength.[17]

On the other hand, when he alone was the one in danger, he wanted to imitate Jesus who went non-violently to his violent death.

> Let us be mild and gentle as the Lamb of God, without weapons to attack or weapons to defend ourselves. We are to let ourselves be bound, shorn, slaughtered, without resisting and without a word of protest.[18]

Undoubtedly his contemplation of the Lamb of God, the lamb of Isaiah 53 that never opened his mouth, led him to write in his rule for the Little Brothers of the Sacred Heart:

> The little brothers are to call to mind each day that one of the gifts their Bridegroom Jesus has graciously bestowed on them is the possibility and the real hope that they may end their lives as martyrs. They are to prepare themselves constantly for this blessed end. They are to act at every moment as befits men who are called by the goodness of the Bridegroom to receive this infinite favor, and perhaps to receive it soon. They are to call down with their desires and their prayers the happy moment when they may give their Beloved the "proof of the greatest love." May every hour find them worthy of such a vocation. And when the moment comes, may they go to meet it without a shadow of self-defense (we are forbidden to possess arms, to bear them or to use them), "like sheep among wolves," meek as the Lamb of God, humble, overflowing with gratitude, praying for their persecutors, determined to let Jesus "make up for what has still to be undergone by Christ" with their deaths. May they offer themselves to him for his greater glory, for all the intentions for which he offered himself on Calvary, uniting the sacrifice of their lives to his own sacrifice, with peace, with blessing and with love, letting him live and act in them more than ever before at this, their supreme hour.[19]

On 1 December 1916, as night was falling, a group of Tuareg rebels arrived at Tamanrasset. They intended to loot the bordj and take the hermit hostage.

They had with them a man Brother Charles knew, and so Brother Charles opened the door without suspicion. He was roughly seized, dragged outside and tied up with ropes.

His attackers went to get Paul Embarek, who lived nearby and used to spend his days at the hermitage. As the only witness to what happened, he always emphasized in his depositions that Brother Charles kept silence throughout the questioning.

The rest happened quickly. As the hermitage was looted, a boy of 15 held Brother Charles under guard. The unexpected arrival of two men on camelback created a moment of panic; the guard lost control and at point-blank range shot his prisoner. Brother Charles died instantly. A few hours before his death, he had written to his cousin:

> When we are reduced to nothing, it is the most powerful means we can have to be united with Jesus and to do good to others. This is what John of the Cross repeated in almost every line he wrote.
>
> When we can suffer and love, we can do much. We can do the most that can be done in this world. We can feel that we are suffering; we cannot always feel that we are loving, and that adds another great suffering! But we know we want to love, and to want to love is to love.[20]

In 1897 at Nazareth, meditating on the death of Jesus, Brother Charles had written these lines. After the kind of death he died, they stand out sharply:

> "And bowing his head, he gave up his spirit." [Jn 19:30] My Lord Jesus, you died and you died for us. If our faith in it were real, how much we would want to die, and to die as martyrs. How much we would want a death in suffering, instead of fearing it.
>
> Whatever may be the reason for which they kill us, if in our souls we receive a cruel and unjust death as a blessed

gift from your hands, if we thank you for it as a welcome grace, as the blessing of imitating your last hours, if we offer it to you as a sacrifice wholeheartedly given, if we do not resist in order that we may obey your words, "Offer the wicked no resistance" [Mt 5:39] and your example, "He was dumb before his shearers and those who led him to the slaughter-house" [Is 53:7], then whatever may be the reason for which they kill us, we will die in pure love. And our death will be a sacrifice of pleasing fragrance. If it is not a martyrdom in the strict sense of the word and in the eyes of other people, it will be one in your eyes and will be a very perfect likeness of your death. For though we may not have offered our blood for our faith in this case, we will with all our might have offered it in sacrifice for your love.[21]

You Will Bear Fruit in Due Season

On 1 January 1908, Brother Charles wrote to Father Huvelin from his hermitage in Tamanrasset:

"Already fifty years old, and I should have something to show for myself and for others. And instead, I am more miserable and useless than ever, and have not accomplished the least good for others. The saying 'You will know them by their fruits' only shows me for what I am."[22]

But in a meditation written in Nazareth in 1897 he expressed a belief that such an apparently sterile life would ultimately bear fruit:

"You tell me that I will be happy with that blessed happiness of the last day … that, as miserable as I am, I am like a palm tree planted beside living waters, the living waters of the Divine Will, Love, and Grace … and that in due season I will bear fruit.

"You deign to console me: you tell me that I shall bear fruit when the time is right. And when will this time be? For each one, this time will be at the Judgment. You promise that as long as I keep trying and stay on the battlefield, even as poor as I may seem in my own eyes, I will have borne fruit on that last day.

"And you add: you will be a beautiful tree with leaves that are eternally green; and all your works will prosper and bear fruit for all eternity. My God, how good you are."[23]

The seed that fell to the ground so silently the evening of 1 December 1916 has borne fruit.

When Brother Charles died, there were about forty lay people who formed the Union of Brothers and Sisters of the Sacred Heart of Jesus, the group he had founded several years before. One of the members, Louis Massignon, felt responsible for sharing Charles de Foucauld's spirituality and asked René Bazin to write a biography to make him known to a wider audience. This publication quickly attracted many followers.

Today, the spiritual family of Charles de Foucauld counts no less than 18 distinct groups, priests, religious women and men, and secular institutes. Through his writings and especially through the vitality of his life, many lay people recognized a Gospel lifestyle that also inspired them to gather as communities for their mutual support and encouragement. In addition, there are large numbers of individuals throughout the world who, without any formal affiliation to these groups, find nourishment in the spirituality of Charles de Foucauld.

They are attracted by the dynamism and relevance of his message for today's world. Due to his own temperament and religious formation, Charles de Foucauld felt a need to write a rule and lay out a precise structure for the life he envisioned. He took his commitment to his vocation as he understood it very seriously.

Despite all of this, he never allowed himself to be boxed in by rigid rules or a caricature of the life of Nazareth. His reference point in living out his intuitions was always the living person of Jesus of Nazareth. The words and deeds of Jesus challenged him throughout the course of his life. He allowed the living Spirit of Jesus, which blows wherever it wills, to constantly direct him in the concrete situations in which he found himself.

A lively faithfulness to his fundamental intuition about Nazareth forged in him a keen attentiveness to the signs of his times and sensitized him to the suffering of others, especially of the "excluded."

Brother Charles' witness remains a challenge to us today. Will we allow the Gospel to speak to us without ceasing in the midst of the situations in which we live, as it did for him? Will we allow the Gospel to shape our entire life and way of being?

This is the word that "does not return void, without accomplishing the work for which it was sent." [Is 53: 10–11] It can make our presence in the world fruitful.

Translation of Brother Charles' Letter to Fr. Huvelin

13 July 1905
About 20° North, near Timiaouin

Very dear Father,

For the first time in a long while I have a chance to get a letter to you. I think of you very often; your child, though such an unworthy one, is very faithful to you.

I'm not forgetting your feast day. Day after tomorrow, on Saint Henry's Day, my poor prayer will be with you even more than usual. Happy Feast Day, beloved father. May the will of JESUS be done in you completely. This is the deep wish, the only wish, I offer you, and it is my prayer for you.

My trip is coming to an end well. I see a good number of local people. The one problem is myself: I am pleased with everything except myself.

Besides my countless shortcomings, there is one thing that bothers me: I wish I could recite the Breviary, have my hours of prayer and meditation and read my little passages of Holy Scripture at least somewhat the way I do when I'm stationary somewhere. And if I try to do it, I have no time left to chat with the Tuaregs or study their language to prepare the way as much as possible for those who will come after me. Since I'm not able to combine the two things, I let the first one go and do only the second, which seems to me the thing God wants most. Even though I think I am doing the right thing, this life without much time devoted exclusively to prayer, this neglect of the pious exercises that do me good and build up my strength, bothers me. I often ask myself if the impossibility of combining the two things is a real one or if it's the result of my lukewarmness.

Thanks be to JESUS, I've been able to celebrate Holy Mass nearly every day. But since I left Beni Abbès, I've almost always replaced the Breviary with the Rosary, and sometimes, putting off the Rosary till the evening, I didn't get through all fifteen decades. When we are on the march, I think about JESUS as much as I can, but sad to say I do it very poorly. When I'm not moving or resting, my time is spent preparing the ways, trying to make friends with the Tuareg and working on the dictionary and translations that will be essential for those who come here to bring JESUS. If I'm wrong to go about it like this, if I should leave off and do it some other way, tell me so and I will obey. In spite of my regrets at being so busy with exterior things, I think — until you tell me to do otherwise — that I am doing the right thing.

As to the future, I need your advice. The people will accept me. But I do not feel they will accept others. As long as no other priests are accepted among the Tuaregs, should I try to settle here, to stay here for a good part of each year? The more I think about it, the more the answer seems to be yes. Somebody has to keep this door open until others can come in by it. Someone has to make friends, build up trust, give a good impression, prepare the ground until the workers get here to till the field. It seems to me more and more that since JESUS, by your guidance, sent me here, I should keep trying to do his work till others get here to replace me.

The little group I'm traveling with will go back to In Salah towards the end of October. Should I go back then to Beni Abbès and not leave it ever again? Should I, on the contrary, settle permanently with the Tuaregs and not leave? Or should I divide my time between Beni Abbès and the Tuaregs until someone comes to replace me in one place or another? I'm inclined to choose the third thing, in spite of the disadvantages to it. For one thing, it makes my life so exterior, and for another thing, there's a question of money. Try to get word to me which of the three choices I should take. You will be obeyed.

Presently I'm trying to build a little house with the Tuaregs. It won't be the beginnings of a fraternity of the Sacred HEART as at Beni Abbès, just a simple shack I can live in. I won't have any land around, neither a lot nor a little; I won't try to cultivate anything. I'll just lead my life of prayer and make ropes and wooden bowls a good part of the year. I'll depend as little as possible on the land.

It's nearly nightfall. Farewell, beloved father. I kneel at your feet and beg you to bless your unworthy child, who loves you and reveres you faithfully with all his heart, in the HEART of our Beloved JESUS,

Br. Ch. of Jesus

Some Dates

15 September 1858	Born at Strasbourg
30 October 1876	Enters military school
June 1881	Campaign against Bou Amana (South Oran District)
March 1882	Resigns from the army
10 June 1883	Begins exploration of Morocco
29 or 30 October 1886	Conversion
16 January 1890	Enters monastery of Our Lady of the Snows
11 July 1890	Arrives at the monastery of Akbes
23 January 1897	Receives permission from Abbot General to leave the Trappist Order
10 March 1897	Taken on as servant to the Poor Clares of Nazareth
9 June 1901	Ordained a priest
28 October 1901	Arrives at Beni-Abbès (South Oran District)
11 August 1905	Settles at Tamanrasset (Hoggar)
1 December 1916	Dies at Tamanrasset

Bibliography

Charles de Foucauld did not write any books, but he did write many personal meditations and many letters to family and friends. Most of these "spiritual writings" have been published (in 17 volumes) by Nouvelle Cité, Paris (from 1973 to 2002).

The following collections of meditations and letters are available in English:

Meditations of a Hermit, London: Burns & Oates, 1930, New York: Orbis Books, 1930.

Sermons in the Sahara, London: Burns & Oates, 1938.

Spiritual Autobiography of Charles de Foucauld, Jean-François Six, New Jersey: Dimension, 1964.

Silent Pilgrimage to God, A Little Brother of Jesus, London: Darton, Longman and Todd, 1974.

Letters from the Desert, London: Burns & Oates, 1977.

Scriptural Meditations on Faith, New York: New City Press, 1988.

Scriptural Meditations on Hope, New York: New City Press, 1990 .

Come, Sing a Song of Love Unknown, Prayers of Charles de Foucauld, New Jersey: Dimension, n.d.

Fifteen Days of Prayer with Charles de Foucauld, Michel Lafont, Missouri: Liguori Press, 1995.

Charles de Foucauld: Selected Writings, Robert Ellsberg, New York: Orbis, 1999.

There are also several biographies, including the following:

Rene Bazin, *Charles de Foucauld: Hermit and Explorer*, London: Burns & Oates, 1923.

George Gorree, *Memories of Charles de Foucauld*, London: Burns & Oates, 1938.

Anne Fremantle, *Desert Calling*, London: Hollis & Carter, 1950.

Michel Carrouges, *Soldier of the Spirit, the Life of Charles de Foucauld*, Victor Gollancz, 1956.

Margaret Trouncer, *Charles de Foucauld*, London: Harrap, 1972.

Elizabeth Hamilton, *The Desert My Dwelling Place*, London: Hodder & Stoughton, 1968.

Charles Lepetit, *Two Dancers in the Desert*, New York: Orbis, 1983.

Philip Hillyer, *Charles de Foucauld*, Collegeville, Minnesota: Liturgical Press, 1990.

Jean-Jacques Antier, *Charles de Foucauld*, San Francisco: Ignatius Press, 1999.

Ali Merad, *Christian Hermit in an Islamic World*, Paulist Press: New Jersey, 1999.

Charles de Foucauld, Catholic Truth Society: London, 2000.

Notes

Introduction

1. Lettre à un Ami de Lycée, Nouvelle Cité 1982, p. 159.

The Years of Unbelief and the Path to Conversion

1. La Derniere place, Nouvelle Cité 1974, p. 100.
2. Letter to H. Duveyrier, 21 February 1892.
3. Lettres à Mme. de Bondy, Desclée de Brouwer 1966, p. 38 (17 April 1892).
4. Lettres à un Ami de Lycée, p. 49.
5. Letter to H. Duvreyier, 21 February 1892.
6. Ibid.
7. La Derniere place, pp. 101–102.
8. Qui peut résister à Dieu, Nouvelle Cité 1980, pp. 30–31.
9. Lettre à un Ami de Lycée, p. 116.
10. Lesourd, La Vraie figure du P. de Foucauld, p. 62 (based on the testimony of Fitz James).
11. Lettres à Henry de Castries, Grattet 1938, p. 86 (8 July 1901).
12. Cahiers Charles de Foucauld 25, p. 38.

13. Lettres à Henry de Castries, p. 95 (14 August 1901).
14. La Derniere place, p. 105.
15. L'Imitation du Bien-aimé, Nouvelle Cité 1997, pp. 78–79.
16. To learn more about Fr. Huvelin, see Un Précurseur, l'Abbé Huvelin, by L. Portier, Cerf 1979.
17. La Derniere place, p. 106.
18. L'imitation du Bien-aimé, p. 79.
19. Ibid.
20. Lettres à Henry de Castries, p. 97 (14 August 1901).
21. La Dernière place, pp. 118–121.
22. See letter to Fr. Huvelin, 22 September 1893.
23. En vue de Dieu seul, Nouvelle Cité 1999, p. 272.
24. Ibid., p. 289.
25. Œuvres Spirituelles de Charles de Jesus père de Foucauld, Seuil 1958, p. 774.

Captivated by Jesus of Nazareth

1. Letter to Fr. Jerome, 21 December 1896, in Cette chère dernière place, Cerf 1991, 147f.
2. Letter to L. de Foucauld, 12 April 1897.
3. Lettres à Mme. de Bondy, p. 60 (24 June 1896).
4. La Derniere place, pp. 50, 53.
5. La Derniere place, p. 54.
6. Voyageur dans la nuit, Nouvelle Cité 1979, p. 208.
7. Lettres à Henry de Castries, p. 97 (14 August 1901).
8. Letter to H. Duvreyier, 24 April 1890.
9. La Dernière place, p. 175.
10. Letter to Fr. Huvelin, 5 November 1890.
11. Lettres à Mme. de Bondy, p. 52 (10 April 1894).
12. Letter to Fr. Huvelin, 22 September 1893.
13. Written at Rome, November 1896, Qui peut resistir à Dieu, pp. 64–65.
14. Letter to Fr. Jerome, in Cette chère dernière place, p. 150f (24 January 1897).
15. Ibid.
16. Letter from Fr. Huvelin, 27 January 1897.

From Nazareth to Beni Abbès

1. Letter to R. de Blic, 25 November 1897.
2. Œuvres Spirituelles, p. 144.
3. L'imitation du Bien-aimé, p. 204.
4. La Derniere place, p. 81.
5. Ibid., p. 41.
6. Letter to Fr. Huvelin, 22 October 1898.
7. Crier l'Evangile, Nouvelle Citè 1974, pp. 18–19.
8. Ibid., pp. 21–22.
9. La Bonté de Dieu, Nouvelle Citè 1996, p. 285.
10. Letter to Fr. Huvelin, 22 October 1898.
11. Letter to Fr. Huvelin, 16 January 1898.
12. Letter to Fr. Huvelin, 26 April 1900.
13. Letter to Fr. Huvelin, 7 May 1900.
14. Letter from Fr. Huvelin to Brother Charles, 20 May 1900.
15. Letter from Fr. Huvelin to Brother Charles, 25 July 1900.
16. See Seul avec Dieu, Nouvelle Citè 1975, p. 77ff.
17. Ibid., p. 83.
18. Letter to Bishop Caron, 8 April 1905.
19. Lettres à Henry de Castries, p. 84f (23 June 1901).
20. Ibid., p. 112f (29 November 1901).
21. Letter to M. de Bondy, 7 January 1902.
22. Letter to Dom Martin, 7 February 1902.
23. Letter to Fr. Huvelin, 15 December 1902.
24. Lettres à Mme. de Bondy, p. 93 (30 December 1901).
25. Letter to M. de Blic, 17 January 1902.
26. Seul avec Dieu, p. 100.
27. Lettres à Mme. de Bondy, p. 109 (21 January 1903).
28. Ibid., p. 110f (2 March 1903).
29. Letter to Fr. Huvelin, 10 June 1903.
30. Lettres à Henry de Castries, p. 118 (15 January 1902).
31. Letter to Dom Martin, in Cette chère dernière place, p. 276f (7 February, 1902).
32. Letter to Bishop Guérin, 28 June 1902.
33. Letter from Bishop Guérin to Brother Charles, 17 September 1902.
34. Letter to Bishop Guérin, 30 September 1902.

35. Letter to Dom Martin, in Cette chère dernière place, p. 17 (17 March 1902).
36. Lettres à Henry de Castries, p. 119 (15 January 1902).
37. Ibid., p. 126 (3 April 1902).
38. Aux Plus Petits de mes Frères, Nouvelle Citè 1973, p. 92–93.
39. Letter to Louis Massignon, 1 August 1916.

A Brother's Presence at the Heart of the Desert

1. Letter from H. Laperrine, June 1903.
2. René Bazin, Charles de Foucauld, Librairie Plon, Paris 1921, p. 268.
3. Letter to Fr. Huvelin, 13 December 1903.
4. Letter to Fr. Huvelin, 17 September 1907.
5. Letter to Fr. Huvelin, 15 July 1904.
6. Carnet de Beni Abbés, Nouvelle Citè 1993, p. 110 (26 May 1904).
7. Ibid., p. 102 (17 May 1904).
8. Carnet de Tamanraset, Nouvelle Citè 1986, p. 46 (22 July 1905).
9. Ibid., p. 48 (11 August 1905).
10. Lettres à Mme. de Bondy, p. 143 (26 August 1905).
11. Letter to Fr. Huvelin, 13 July 1905.
12. Letter to Fr. Huvelin, 4 December 1909.
13. Letter to Bishop Guérin, 2 July 1907.
14. Letter to Fr. Huvelin, 15 July 1906.
15. Letter to Fr. Huvelin, 1 January 1908.
16. Lettres à Mme. de Bondy, p. 160 (17 July 1907).
17. Ibid., 164f (25 December 1907).
18. Letter to M. de Bondy, 26 January 1908.
19. Letter to M. de Bondy, January 1908.
20. Letter to Fr. Voillard, 12 Janurary 1912.
21. Carnet de Tamanrasset, pp. 188–189 (1909).
22. Quoted by L. Lehureaux in Aux Sahara avec le Père de Foucauld, Saint-Paul 1946, p. 115.
23. Lettres à Mme. de Bondy, p. 147 (16 December 1905).
24. Lettres à Henry de Castries, p. 193f (10 December 1911).

25. Lettres à Mme. de Bondy, p. 189 (16 June 1910).

26. Ibid., p. 198f (9 July 1911).

27. Ibid., p. 200 (15 August 1911).

28. Ibid., p. 236 (16 April 1915).

29. Letter to Bishop Guérin, 27 February 1903.

30. Letter to J. Hours, 3 May 1912.

In the Likeness of Jesus Even Unto Death

1. Lettres à Mme. de Bondy, p. 227 (17 March 1914).

2. Ibid., p. 229 (20 July 1914).

3. La Bonté de Dieu, p. 194.

4. Letter to Fr. Huvelin 8 February 1900.

5. Letter to Bishop Guérin, 15 January 1908.

6. Lettres à Mme. de Bondy, p. 231 (15 September 1914).

7. Letter to Laperrine, 14 December 1914.

8. Lettre à un Ami de Lycée, 25 November 1914.

9. See Carnet de Beni Abbès, p. 150–151.

10. Quoted by René Bazin, in Charles de Foucauld, p. 466.

11. Lettres à Mme. de Bondy, p. 57f (19 February 1896).

12. Ibid., p. 59 (24 June 1896).

13. Voyageur dans la nuit, p. 35.

14. Seul avec Dieu, p. 103.

15. Voyageur dans la nuit, pp. 177.

16. Letter to H. Laperrine, 1 July 1916.

17. Aux Plus Petits de Mes Frères, p. 131–132.

18. L'Imitation du Bien-aimé p. 146.

19. Règlement et Directoire, Nouvelle Citè 1995, pp. 305–306.

20. Lettres à Mme. de Bondy, pp. 251f (1 December 1916).

21. Vue de Dieu seul, pp. 217–218.

22. Lettre à l'abbé Huvelin, 1 January 1908.

23. Qui peut résister à Dieu, p. 109.